The Arringtons
in
Bolivia

Mrs. Bob L. White

—Missions Around the World—
Series

The Arringtons in Bolivia

Mrs. Bob L. White

Baptist Progress
P. O. Box 2085
Waxahachie, Texas 75168
Phone 972-923-0756

Scripture quotations are based on the King James Version
of the Bible.

The Arringtons in Bolivia

Introduction

Introduction

The Arringtons in Bolivia is the story of two people who followed the plan of God for their lives. By faith they staked a claim in the Bolivian jungle for the Lord. A church stands today as a testimony of the power of God in the lives of men and women who are totally committed to Him.

The trials and triumphs of the Arrington Family arouse various emotions in the reader. One could cry at times because of the trials they faced, but one can rejoice when the blessings out weigh the problems, and victory is won by trust in the Lord.

First-hand accounts of their adventures are gathered from articles written by Bro. and Mrs. Arrington for *The Gleaner*, (BMAA Missions Magazine) and from information supplied by Mrs. Arrington and Mary Jane. They are not in chronological order but are arranged to picture various aspects of their ministry.

Many co-workers labored with the Arringtons. Americans and Bolivians worked side-by-side to build airstrips, "cut-in" to the jungle, navigate up and down the river, build homes, a clinic, churches, and carry on a medical ministry. The work was a partnership between the Arringtons and other missionaries, BMAA people in the United States, the Bolivian believers, and the Lord.

Part I
The Missionaries

The unseen hand of the Lord drew a courageous couple together. A chance meeting led to love, marriage, and a family. The call to a foreign mission field came, they answered. They were not seeking adventure and excitement but found both. Following the leadership of the Lord, the trail led to challenges and victories in the jungles of Bolivia.

M. S., Mary Jane, and Katherine Arrington 1971

Mary Jane, Katherine, and M. S.

Chapter 1
A Boy and a Girl

Melvin Slay Arrington (Deek as he was affectionately known by family and close friends) was born January 23, 1919 in Hattiesburg, Mississippi to Moses S. and Eulalia A. Arrington. He graduated from Hattiesburg High School in 1938 then attended Jackson Commercial College and studied to be an accountant. He was in the military in World War II serving in the Pacific after basic training.

Annie Katherine Byrd was born in March 7, 1924 in Mize, Mississippi to loving, God-fearing parents, Henry Hamilton and Leona Byrd. She recalls a happy childhood as the youngest of nine children. She has pleasant memories of going to a Presbyterian church near their family home. She was saved when she was twelve years old. Her paternal grandparents, who lived with them, were members of a missionary Baptist church.

Katherine attended the same school from grades one through 12 in Mize. After graduation in 1942 she moved to Jackson, Mississippi to find employment. She worked at several different jobs, but she was not happy in any of them. She entered a three year course of nursing in Jackson in the spring of 1943. Nurses were not allowed to be married and continue in training, but that posed no problem as she was interested only in becoming a nurse. She became a Registered Nurse in 1946 and began working in a hospital.

Chapter 2
A Romance and Marriage

Deek and Katherine's paths crossed after he returned from military service and began to work as an accountant, and she began her career as a registered nurse. Was it really by chance they met? No, it was the hand of the Lord!

A hospital nursing supervisor asked Katherine to go to the White House Boarding House, across from the state capital building in Jackson, to administer intravenous medication to an elderly patient. The patient's daughter arranged for Katherine's transportation for the "house call." Melvin Arrington was the driver, and although Katherine had not met him before, she felt safe since he was sent by the patient's family. After the "house call" treatment, Deek requested permission to see Katherine home. Their friendship soon developed into a romance. They were married in the home of Dr. W. A. Huett, pastor of First Baptist Church, Jackson on September 11, 1948 and began their lives together.

The Arrington home was blessed by the arrival of their children. Melvin Slay, Jr. (Buddy) was born at the end of the first year of marriage and daughter, Mary Jane was born about six years later.

Bro. M. S. was saved in the spring of 1957. Bro. Ray Thornton relates this story:

A man stopped by where I was working on the church building and introduced himself as M. S. Arrington. He told me he had bought a home down the street and was interested in the church for his children and asked me if I would accept a donation on the church. While we were talking, I asked him if he were saved, and he said he had joined a church when he was young, but didn't feel he was saved at the time he joined the church. I witnessed to him at that time. The following week two deacons went by to visit with him. He told them he and his family would be at church that Sunday. (Bro. M. S. gave his heart to the Lord later that week.) The following week during our revival in which Bro. Vern Holifield was preaching, he and his wife came for baptism. The date was April 17, 1957. They were baptized that Sunday evening and became members of Bethel, Jackson, Mississippi. Bro. Arrington and Katherine went to work immediately in the church. He served as church clerk and taught Sunday School for about two years. On March 10, 1959, he made known his call to the ministry.

Katherine was faced with a new challenge—could she be a minister's wife? Although she felt unworthy, she had a desire to do her best. She was thankful God had answered her prayers for her family.

Bro. Arrington felt the need to prepare to serve the Lord. He entered Mississippi College in Clinton, Mississippi to further his theological training. His employer allowed him to work and attend classes, too. He worked, studied, and pastored a church 75 miles away. After graduation he and his family moved to Jacksonville, Texas so he could attend the

Baptist Missionary Association Theological Seminary. He graduated in 1966.

M. S. lights Coleman lantern before dark (May 1978)

Chapter 3
A Clear Call Answered

Bro. Arrington recognized his call to missions during his college years, but wanted to prepare first, then seek God's will for the field where they would serve. One day, when he could keep it to himself no longer, he poured out his heart to Katherine, telling her of his call to the missions field and of his desire to go. She listened carefully. She thought they might be able to serve on an interstate field and that would not be so far away. They were already eight hours away from home, so it couldn't be much further, she reasoned. But he said, "No, God wants us to go to a foreign country."

Katherine knew she would have to pray much about this move, as she did not feel a clear call as did Deek. She did pray earnestly, remembering that she had committed her life to God, but still wondering what she could do on a mission field. She was not a teacher; she was a nurse, mother, and housewife. As she prayed, God revealed to her people need physical help as well as spiritual, especially in under-developed countries where so little medical care is available.

Katherine didn't get a definite answer until Bro. M. S. made public his call. When he went forward, she followed, willing to go wherever the Lord sent him.

Bro. Arrington made application to the Baptist Missionary Association of America to be a foreign missionary. He had looked forward to this day, his education behind him, his call clear and urgent. Imagine his surprise when the personnel committee did not recommend him for election! The deciding factor seemed to be he was 46. Bro. Arrington was so sure the Lord was calling him and was so determined to follow that call, he questioned the reason for their decision. The committee invited Bro. and Mrs. Arrington to meet at the next scheduled meeting, where they were questioned extensively. The Lord changed the decision of the committee, and the Arringtons were recommended and elected to work among the Indians of Bolivia, South America.

Chapter 4
The Destination—Bolivia

Bro. M. S., Katherine, and Mary Jane left Jackson, Mississippi airport Friday, August 18, 1967. (Buddy stayed in Mississippi with his grandmother to attend college). They flew from Jackson to Atlanta, then Miami, Panama City (with an over-night layover), and finally arrived in La Paz, Bolivia. Obtaining resident visas took a week in La Paz. On Saturday, August 26 the Arringtons went to Santa Cruz. They would study the language and prepare for their jungle ministry in this frontier city on the edge of the tropics.

Bro. Arrington described Santa Cruz this way:

Until ten years ago Santa Cruz was isolated from the rest of the country. Now it is like a bustling town of the early wild west. Planes land here and a road (of sorts) has been opened from Cochabamba over the mountains, and people are coming. This town and surrounding area is being developed through the aid of the United States government and others who are trying to tap the vast resources in this underdeveloped country of Bolivia. . . . The climate in the Santa Cruz area is hot except when the cool dust-laden "surrazo" wind blows from the south during the dry season and piles deep sand dunes on the old brick sidewalks. It has been windy and sandy both since we came.

The "foreigners" were quite a puzzle to the native people. Why would the North Americans leave their home in the United States where there were roads, cars, airplanes, and television sets? Why would they choose this neighborhood to make their home?

The people who came to Bolivia with the oil companies lived to themselves. Their maids and other servants did their buying in the market, and they had little contact with the people of the city. Not so with this strange family, for they were continually talking with the Bolivians. They didn't drink, attend the wild parties they heard of other North Americans having, and they didn't speak Spanish. The strangest thing of all was a Book they talked about all the time. Always there was talk of Christ, who died for our sins. Some of the natives had heard of the Bible, but one had not been available to them before.

The Arrington's rented a house and began housekeeping with a small amount of furniture. Their landlady was a Bolivian lady who helped Katherine shop and taught her how to prepare vegetables to make them safe to eat. They waited five months before their shipment of household goods arrived. When the shipment finally came, it had been broken into and some of their things were stolen. Bro. Arrington commented on the loss of their goods:

I can think of at least two things right away concerning this experience that has helped us. One thing is patience. The Bible speaks a good deal about learning patience. The other thing is to remember Jesus' teachings on forgiveness. For those who rifled and stole our belongings we ask God to forgive them and in some way we pray and trust that those very objects may in some miraculous way be used of God to convert their souls. Why, I'd give all the shipment and every possession of mine on this earth for one soul, but this is not God's plan of salvation. It is through Jesus alone, (Acts 4:12), so we are asking God to convict and save them.

Everything was much different here than back in the United States. Even the mail was slow, and six weeks went by before the first letters arrived from home.

Bro. Arrington and Katherine both attended language school. While they were studying Spanish, they were also learning the customs of the country. The study was very hard and Katherine thought to be able to speak Spanish as the natives did, their tongues needed to be loose on both ends. They were blessed to find a school for Mary Jane. The Santa Cruz Cooperative School was an American-Bolivian school taught in English. Mary Jane could study Spanish there, too.

They invited their neighbors and every new acquaintance to worship services in their home. Emeterio Mendosa and his wife were the first ones to attend and be saved. The group grew slowly, and the Bethel Baptist Church (Iglesia Bautista Betel) was organized later from the mission.

They were busy witnessing and winning souls the two years they were living in Santa Cruz, but their goal was to move to the jungle.

Part II
The Country, Bolivia
The Lord led them to a strange country to minister. They worked together to learn as much as they could about the land, the people, and travel.

Santa Cruz, Bolivia
Dirt street through main part of city
where we lived first two years of work.

Chapter 1
A Land of Contrasts

Bolivia was named for the South American liberator, Simon Bolivar. It is the fifth largest South American country in area and very rich in natural resources, especially minerals such as tin, silver, copper, lead, and zinc.

The Amazon jungles, the dry plains of the Chaco, and the Andes Mountains are natural barriers which shut Bolivia from the rest of the world. It is bordered on the north and east by Brazil; on the west, by Chili and Peru; and on the south, by Paraguay and Argentina. In the west are the rugged Andes mountains with a year around cold climate, known as the Altiplano or high plateau area. The Andean range at its widest in Bolivia is some 400 miles. The Western Cordillera, the formidable barrier which separates Bolivia from Chili, has high peaks of between 19,000 and 21,420 feet and a number of active volcanoes along its crest. The passes across it are above 13,000 feet. Although the Altiplano covers only ten percent of the total area of the country, nearly 75% of the population live there and the major cities are located there. Bolivia has the world's highest capital city, La Paz, at 12,400 feet above sea level, and highest navigable lake, Lake Titicaca.

The area to the east is the middle section of the country known as the Yungas or Valleys. The tropical lowlands are drained by the Amazon River. The altitude is only 500 to 2500 feet. Rainfall is seasonal, and large stretches suffer from alternate flooding and drought. Occasional cold, dust-laden winds from the south—the surrazos—lower the temperature considerably. In the north and east the Oriente has dense tropical forests, covering about 200,000 square miles.

Bolivia has no seacoast of its own which is a great hindrance to Bolivia's trade. Goods intended for shipment overseas can be shipped by railroad or by river boat, but they must cross foreign territory before they reach the coast.

Shopping in the open market in Santa Cruz.

In Santa Cruz near where we lived. Homemade oxcarts pulled by oxen, at that time the usual mode of travel bringing produce to town.

Chapter 2
A People of Varied Cultures

One thousand years ago Bolivia was a part of the fabled Inca Empire. Today the ruins of the great early civilization and many of the Incas' descendants can be seen. There are two main groups of Bolivian people—the Spanish-speaking people who are of European ancestry, a small minority, and the Indians, who make up the larger population group and speak their own languages. Differences in education, language, habits, and culture divide them. Although they are fewer in number, the upper class has dominated the economic, social, and political life since the Spanish conquest over four hundred years ago.

Living conditions in Bolivia were primitive when the Arringtons arrived in the capitol city, La Paz. The Altiplano Indians lived in adobe huts with thatched roofs and no windows. Altiplano women wore colorful skirts (sometimes as many as six at once), and black cloth derby hats set squarely on their heads. They carried burdens in papoose style, just as they did their babies. Most farmers used wooden plows and other simple tools.

The Indian markets in the lowlands (Santa Cruz) which sold the produce of the area, were interesting. Meat hung out in the open, covered with flies. There were fruits, vegetables, nuts, and a variety of items which were unfamiliar. Drinking water was very scarce. Bottled water could be purchased for one and one-half to two pesos (12-17¢ U. S money). Water from anywhere else had to be boiled and filtered, and vegetables had to be washed in a solution to make them safe to eat.

The stores, restaurants, and the houses were open, that is, they were not screened, and there were many flies and mosquitoes.

The Quechua and Aymara, two large groups of Indians, and several smaller groups have survived from the ancient Incas. The Arringtons worked with the Yuracare tribe, which is one of the smaller groups of Indians who live in the tropical forests. They numbered 1500 people in 1800, less than 1000 by 1900, and today they exceed 2500. They are gentle people who live in small groups, sometimes less than 100.

In 1760 Roman Catholic missionaries made the first attempt to bring Christianity to the Yuracares. The missionary effort was not successful, but the Indians learned the Spanish language, which they speak today, in addition to their native dialect. Two hundred and nine years later Bro. Arrington was able to communicate with them because they could speak Spanish.

Native customs, folklore, language, beliefs, and handicrafts have been preserved and are practiced today. Bolivia is generally lacking in education although there are schools in the towns. It is said that 70% of the population is illiterate.

Bro. Arrington made the following observation soon after arriving in Bolivia in late 1967:

Recently we made a trip about thirty miles to the north on the only road going north that is passable the year around that I know of. It is paved for about thirty or forty miles north and from then on it is by river when the river beds have sufficient water. As one goes farther north the rivers are larger as they wind their way to a convergence forming the Madeira river which is the largest tributary of the Amazon. As far as the road goes one can see, mile after mile, land that is unused and is covered with tropical growths. Indian mud huts are scattered here and there. Further to the north, along the rivers, there are many tribes so we are told. Efforts to reach many of these tribes have been made by Wycliffe Translators and New Tribes Missions. We are told that this is a slow and tedious task because the Indian tribes, at least those who have had any contact at all with the white man, only know him as an exploiter and enemy. Of course, this is true because many of the contacts made by traders and drifters were for selfish and personal gain. Many tribes that have not become civilized no doubt have heard of the exploitation of their people and are fearful and many times take a hostile attitude toward the white man. Time is required to win the confidence of these people who have been isolated from the world, as we know it, for centuries.

On this trip we were told, by a missionary, of fierce Indian tribes all along the rivers leading north. This man worked in a part of the vast area along one of the rivers at one time and told just how white traders and drifters had exploited the Indians. When these unprincipled men would see the Indians along the banks of the river in their brief waist bands or no clothing at all, holding their spears and blow guns, would shoot them as they would a wild animal. One can see why the Indians who have not been reached with the Gospel have no confidence in the white man as most of their experiences with him have been unpleasant and detrimental to his well-being.

19

One can read of the experiences of others who have reached the Indians with the Gospel and rejoice in miraculous conversions from savage to saint.

Homes of Indians along the Chapare River.

Typical Yuracare Indian—one of oldest in group with which we worked.

A Yuracare mother with her baby.

Chapter 3
A Challenge, Travel by River into the Jungle

Travel in Bolivia was a challenge every step of the way. Main roads linking the big cities were paved. Beyond the roads man had to travel on the rivers, when there was enough water to navigate. The changes in the seasons from rainy to dry often changed the path of the rivers and shut off the regular routes. Days were busy with the language study, witnessing, and learning the customs of a new land. The future work among the Indians in the jungles was never far from Bro. Arrington's mind. He decided to make a survey trip to learn more. He wrote of his experiences on a survey trip:

The survey trip through the jungles to the north by river took 33 days. Traveling in the Bolivian jungles is uncertain in many respects, but I felt the Lord's presence. Once we left Santa Cruz for the tropical lowlands, we expected all means of communication to be cut off until we could reach a town with an airport or short wave radio. Quite by chance I was able to send a letter home after 15 days out. We passed a

21

canoe in the middle of the Mamore River near Trinidad. The canoe was going to the port nearest Trinidad, and I gave one of the people in the canoe the letter and some money and asked them to mail it in Trinidad.

We began our trip in a rented jeep, loaded with our equipment. Necessary items were motor, tarpaulin, a 50 gallon drum of gasoline, cans of oil, kerosene, bedrolls, lanterns, guns and ammunition, rations, medicines, etc. The first leg of the trip was to the Yapacani because I needed to be acquainted with this area also. I stayed with the equipment while waiting for the boat to be pulled to the river from nearby where it had been built. There were many curious onlookers who examined the motor and asked many questions. One fellow asked me why we were going down the Yapacani River. He told me of the many shallows to cross and warned me of the savages north of there. Well, I didn't fancy the idea of dragging the boat over the sands in the shallows, but his face became puzzled when I told him we were looking for Indians and wanted to make friends with them. We believe in a new birth and know God will give a man a new life when he repents and truly believes whether savage or civilized.

Although the rivers and jungles present problems to transportation they hold a wealth of scenery and wild life. The caiman or alligator is hunted throughout the course of the rivers. There are many kinds of fish, many large ones that are edible. We could see them sometimes ahead of us in the shallow water as they would surface and make waves and a swirling of the water. River dolphin can be seen as far south as Puerto Grether. Large and small river turtles are to be found and along the banks can be seen the river seal, coypou, otter, and the capybara or swimming river-hog that runs along and suddenly plunges into and disappears below the surface of the water. There is a danger from electric eels, rayas, or sting rays that can inflict a serious wound with a ferocious saw-edged string in its tail. The forest is the home of the jaguar (called tigre), wild pig, monkey, ant-eater, badger, sloth, tapir (South American elephant) and many others. Birds include wild duck, turkey, toucans, lorro (parrots of all different sizes), perdiz, and many other water fowl.

Some trees are covered with needle-sharp thorns and a feeling of shock runs through a person when he might, by mistake, grab hold of the wrong tree. Then other trees are the home of certain ants. One tree in particular has 'palo diablos' (wood devils) that can sting worse than any other. Several of them can put a person in a bad shape. It is necessary to know this tree and to avoid it, taking care not to jar it because the ants will shower down upon one who is passing under.

One afternoon we saw some activity up ahead. At first we thought it might be savages, and Emeterio told me I had better get the gun or at least put it in view. Many of these people, at least in the jungles and along the borders where there is lawlessness, respect a gun. I told Emeterio my guns were for protection against snakes, wild animals, and for getting food. I have long ago asked the Lord to help me to rely upon Him for strength and protection when and if He permits me to face an uncivilized people.

I feel my survey trip was a success. It was a hard one but profitable. I traveled nearly a 1000 miles by river going north alone, the longest navigable distance north and south in Bolivia. I was able to locate three different groups of Yuras Indians. There were so many sick along the way I turned out to be a medical missionary also, a poor one I am sure, but the best they had. I witnessed to many people while away and distributed many Spanish tracts also.

River scene as we travel along.
Sand bar with trees and jungle growth in background.

Bolivia travel.

Part III
Help from Near and Far

The Arringtons made friends with the people in Santa Cruz. They began a mission in their home, and gradually they were able to win men and women to the Lord. Mary Jane completed her first year in school. Her school work and grades were very good.

If they were to go into the jungles to live, they would need several things such as a guide, a means of communication, and a boat on which they could live, transport goods, and travel. Just as Bro. Arrington believed, God provided all their needs.

Deek and Mary Jane (January 1969).
Deek's first birthday in Bolivia. Cake made from scratch
and just as proud as if it came from a bakery.

Mary Jane with her pet monkey.
Day after returning
from second survey trip.

Our daughter,
Mary Jane, in the jungle with us.

Chapter 1
A Native Guide

Bro. Arrington learned many lessons of survival during the survey trips. His preparations to move were his first priority. To carry out his plan, he had to build a boat on which to live, travel, and transport supplies. He would need a guide to help him find his way in the jungle. He wrote concerning his hopes:

Our language school time is passing fast in these last few months, and it will soon be time for us to make the transition we have long waited for—to launch out into a full time work in the remote areas for the Master.

We have some disappointments in life, but in our work for the Lord, most of all, we want to fight the good fight of faith. By His grace and power we are trusting Him to give us the victory. Ours is a Gospel mission with the words of life and even the medical part of our work is a means to an end, and that end is the salvation of souls. Travel is slow and uncertain, and the only way to travel in the jungles, besides walking, is by river, especially when one needs to move supplies, family, etc., and to establish a mission. Of course, there is the possibility of ox cart or horses if there happens to be a trail or the possibility of making one where you want to go. Then there is plane travel to and from major points, but it is too expensive and, of course, spans these isolated people in the jungles who need Jesus as their Saviour. To reach these people is my work God has called me to do.

Brethren, the last remote corners of the earth are fast being reached, and everything points to the imminent return of Christ to this earth. There is unbelief on every hand. False doctrine has been spread like wildfire. Satan leads the masses today in a false religion. My prayer is that God will give me wisdom and strength to reach some of these people that have not been reached.

Bro. Arrington was getting ready for the big move out to the jungle. He needed the help of someone with experience in the jungle. Bro. Arrington introduces his first helper:

Mario had come by my house several times when I was building the boat. A friend, Rolando, had told him about the mission, his conversion, and our mission to the savages. Mario had lived and hunted in the jungle most of his life, and he told me he was a friend of a man named David who was a member of the missionary group mentioned in <u>Commandos for Christ</u> by Bruce Porterfield, who was killed by the Indians on the Itenez River which is the Bolivian-Brazilian frontier. He said he had been a paid worker of this group at one time and was even baptized. Mario wanted to go as a paid guide, but since his motive was different from ours, my interest waned. However, I had just about decided to hire him on a temporary basis at least until he could put me on some Indian trails, that is if I could get in touch with him again. (Just a few days later, after a chance meeting in downtown Santa Cruz, Mario was invited to the Arrington home where he accepted the Lord as his Saviour.)

Our paths crossed in downtown Santa Cruz. I

invited Mario to come home with us, and I led him to the Lord. Now he wants to volunteer his service to the Lord. Praise God! How mighty is His hand to help us. Now I have another brother in Christ to help me. I feel much better having brethren in Christ on such a mission. On the following Sunday Mario made public his profession.

Our BMA airplane lands on the Chapare Air Strip
to bring some food and other supplies such as medicine for the people.

Chapter 2
A Way of Communication

Always when there is a need, the Lord has the plan already worked out, just waiting for someone to put it into action. That someone in this case was Bro. Craig Branham. A little more than a year after the Arringtons moved to Santa Cruz, Bro. Branham, Director of Missions, made a visit to Bolivia. He gave this account of his visit:

When I arrived in Bolivia, I was met by the Arringtons. Although I have read every article, and felt I knew the situation there, I was surprised—surprised at being in the very edge of the jungle, surprised at the headway made and planning that have been done by the Arringtons. Yes, and I must admit being surprised too at the great courage of the Arringtons.

Santa Cruz is located between some rivers which make up the headwaters of the Amazon. Along the streets which have been paved in only the last few months, you can see Indians from time to time. Then only a few miles north toward the Amazon there is a triangle of land formed by the merging of two rivers. In this triangle lives a tribe of uncivilized Indians. They have never been reached by white men. They still worship animals in their heathen rituals. It is with this tribe Bro. Arrington wishes to work.

Our Bolivian missionary knows this will not be a quick job. It will not be an easy one, either. There will be many years of painstaking effort before they can be reached and some of them won.

As I listened while Bro. Arrington talked of his recent trip which had taken him into the waters of the rivers flowing by this Indian inhabited triangle, my heart was touched. He told of his experiences. He told of some of his apprehensions, yes, and fears. Then as he talked, he spoke of his aspirations and determination to go where the Lord has led. He said, 'We know there are dangers and hardships. We know there is the need for a plane and some radio contact. We are praying the Lord will give it. In the meantime, we know our God is able to protect and provide for us.

Bro. Branham left Bolivia with a great burden. When he returned to the United States, he wrote the following in *The Gleaner*:

In order to give the kind of back-up that is needed, we will need to buy an airplane for Bolivia. We will need to get radio equipment. It will cost money, a lot of money. God will provide it for us if we will give it for His cause. Never in the almost 13 years in your missions office have I felt a greater need.

Present plans are for them to leave Santa Cruz by boat as soon as their language study is finished. They will go to where the Yapacani and Palacio Rivers merge. How will they live? There are no houses, except for the huts in which the Indians live, so they must build a home. It will be constructed of bamboo and covered with thatch unless or until they can get lumber or other building materials. However, this seems unlikely. There will be no electricity, no running water, and none of the modern conveniences. The only school for Mary Jane will be a

31

correspondence course. Food will have to be secured locally. At present, access will be only by river. It will take a week to go to the Post Office and return. Most of the time there will be no contact with the civilized world, except for the occasional boats which will come up river.

As I listened I became burdened. When I think of the possibilities of sickness and the need to get out and to medical help, I am burdened for us to have someone there to help them. When I think of the possibility of unfriendly Indians, or even those who are partially civilized becoming angry, I become so burdened I can hardly bear to think of their being there alone without any help in case they need it.

Most of our people know Bro. Marvin Loyd and his family returned earlier this year from Nicaragua so Mrs. Loyd could complete her education, and they could better serve as self-paid missionaries. My burden became so great I talked with Bro. Loyd about it. Learning of the conditions there, he, too, became burdened. He is willing to go.

Bro. Loyd is the logical person for the task. He has already been approved by the Missionary Personnel Committee. He has served our Association in Nicaragua as a self-paid missionary for more than a year. He already knows some of the language. He is also familiar with the need and value of missionary aviation. Feeling the need for this work in Nicaragua, he bought a plane there and gave it to the Association. He holds both Nicaraguan and American pilot's licenses. To do the work which needs to be done, the Loyds will again have to sacrifice. She has not yet finished her degree as she had planned. Yet, they are both ready and willing to make whatever sacrifices are necessary so they can serve the Lord. How thankful we should be for such dedicated young people!

In order to give the kind of back-up that is needed, we will need to buy an airplane for Bolivia. We will need to get radio equipment.

The radios will give us daily contact between our two brethren. The plane will enable help to be into the jungle for them if needed in less than an hour and a half.

The Missionary Committee shared the burden with Bro. Branham and voted to send Bro. and Mrs. Marvin Loyd to Bolivia and to authorize a fund for a plane and radios for the work. The Arringtons rejoiced when they received the news. Money was quickly raised for the plane and equipment.

In *The Gleaner* (February 1969), Bro. Loyd wrote:

Last month we purchased the plane. It is a Cessna Skylark with all the equipment we will need with the exception of large wheels for soft field landings. Bro. Earl Horton of Lubbock has given the plane a complete inspection and a top overhaul, so as soon as the papers for the nose wheel conversion are on hand, we can finish equipping it for the jungle.

Bro. Marvin Loyd and his family went to Bolivia early in the spring of 1969. They had been able to get the plane in with relatively little time and expense.

Bro. Marvin and Bro. Arrington went to work right away. They made four flights over the rivers and jungles in search of a base camp. On the last flight they had agreed Puerto Palos would be the best site for a base camp at least to begin. Puerto Palos is an abandoned oil company site. There was a landing strip there that they could put in use by doing a little work on it. At least it seemed to be suitable as they flew low over it. There is nothing else there, but this strip meant a lot. The other campos or clearings were standing in water, and the only alternative would be to cut out a strip.

Chapter 3
A Boat for the Journey

Bro. Arrington worked several months to build the boat. He named it War-Ark in honor of the people in Warren, Arkansas who raised the money to pay for it. He relates this experience:

Many curious onlookers have passed and watched the gradual building of the boat in our yard which is a long way from the river. An American missionary who has been in Santa Cruz for three and one-half years was leaving for the States and came by to say goodbye and to wish us well. In a jesting manner he said the rains were beginning to come, and he wanted to get on the 'ark.' I told him, 'Alright there were five in his family and three in mine, and that made eight.' He said we picked the hardest work in Bolivia and would have many to discourage us even Americans. He didn't know we had already heard this. However, I told him we didn't pick the work but were called to it. I have been told by several the unreached savages of Bolivia are the most barbarous in the world but I shall not be moved. I admit my fears, but I feel they are normal. I believe God will give the needed grace. Unless we could say we were willing to give our lives for those people and for the sake of our Lord, I don't believe He would use us anyway. I am glad to be sent to these people and bring them the message of salvation in Jesus. Who knows? Some of these people may never hear about Jesus again.

The boat was about six feet wide and 25 feet long with a room built for shelter and protection in the jungle and with shelves where medicines could be stored. It was painted dark green and trimmed in white with two large white crosses painted on either side of the boarded walls of the room. The room was screened with heavy wooden doors at either end with padlocks. There were four screened and shuttered windows which could be locked from the inside.

When the time came to launch the boat, it was taken over land by truck about 80 miles northwest of Santa Cruz to the Yapacani landing. The trip down river to the prospective base camp would take three or four days. Puerto Palos was an abandoned oil company site with a landing strip that could be put in use with less work than other sites they had considered.

The river was gradually falling, and unless they moved the boat immediately, the chances were they might have to leave it until the rainy season a year later. They quickly moved the boat down to kilometer 24 where the possibility of navigation was much better. The boat was left there to await the final day of departure.

Building boat ("War-Ark") in our
back yard in Santa Cruz (November 1968).

Part IV
New Surroundings

At last the Arringtons were able to move into the jungle. They had learned the language, gathered the necessary supplies, employed a guide, built a house-boat, and had communication support. Now they would be able to live and work with the Indians. God had put the burden into their hearts, and He would work through them day by day.

Boat and canoe loaded with supplies.

Chapter 1
A Trip Down The River

The day of departure finally arrived. The following is a first-hand account of the trip from Santa Cruz to the jungle location:

Our party of five—Rolando, Mario, Katherine, Mary Jane and I—left Santa Cruz Monday, March 31, 1969 at 2:30 p.m. headed for our jungle mission work on a truck loaded to the brim. Part of our cargo was chickens, Reina (Queen) our jungle dog, Gatito (little cat), two lorros (parrots), and even some pepper plants. My friends in the States will remember how I loved hot pepper; well, there is plenty in Bolivia. From Santa Cruz we went some 75 miles to the northwest to the turn-off for San Juan and continued down a dirt road for 24 kilometers to a trail which leads into the river. The driver said nothing until we got to this point, but now I could tell it looked pretty bad to him. At times the truck swayed to and fro with such violence when it hit a low, marshy place, it seemed the kerosene refrigerator we were trying to take would be broken. I was up front and nearly thrown off or brushed off by overhanging limbs until I decided to abandon the cargo to its own fate since Katherine and Mary Jane were in a safe place within the cab and Rolando was on the rear. Dark was falling fast, so Mario and I ran up ahead of the truck trying to find the best route. The driver had already turned on his lights.

By the time we got to the end of the trail at the river's bluff, it was completely dark. We began the task of unloading because the driver and his two helpers wanted to get out. Our clothes were completely wet with perspiration, and the mosquitoes were literally chewing us up. Poor Katherine! I later discovered her forehead was covered with whelps. In the jungle north of Santa Cruz one never knows when it might rain and, since it was threatening, we covered everything as best we could with a tarpaulin. There were deep ravines in the jungle growth between the cliff and the river's edge. Katherine fell going through this, but like a good soldier she got up and continued through the brambles to the boat.

Before day it began to rain and continued through the day. Our problem now was to move our equipment we brought by truck on down river since our boat could not carry it all. We were told a nearby hunter by the name of Carmelo was down river hunting and probably would help us. We decided it would be best to wait on him. While waiting here Mario, Rolando, and I along with two other men began taking the things down the high bluff we were going to load on our boat. We built a type of sled out of balsa logs and strapped the refrigerator to it and fastened a 1" rope to the box and sled and lowered it over the cliff about 50 feet to the boat. The kerosene stove and washing machine (which we hope to use if we can get the generator) were lowered in the same manner. The other boxes and crates we hustled down on our backs.

Carmelo arrived in the afternoon in another small boat and told us he had trouble with his motor but if he could get a replacement from someone back at the Yapacani port, he would help us the next day. The next morning we went down the road to Carmelo's hut only to find out he could not get the replacement. However, the men who had brought him up river were going to return downstream with supplies for some oil company workers and agreed to help us for a price and 20 liters of gasoline. I seized this opportunity and loaded on all they would let me. The rest we had to stack somewhere on our already overloaded boat. At this time we still had all of our animals except Gatito who escaped to the woods, and we weren't able to retrieve him. I suppose Mary Jane felt this loss more than any of us although all of us, I think, had become attached to him.

The other boat went on ahead of us. One of the men told me their workers were without food and supplies, and they needed to go on. They were going to Parker-Gulf Oil Company Camp near Puerto Palos. Their "pista" (landing strip) is nearby, and we plan to stop there temporarily in order to hold contact with Bro. Marvin once a week. From Puerto Palos we plan to go down river another day or two. We are not sure just yet exactly how far down river we will go, but we believe our opportunity to cut across the jungle to near the Chori river will be better from that point.

We left kilometer 24 around 2:30 p.m., April 4, and traveled until dark. We anchored for the night in the mouth of a small creek that entered the Yapacani on our right. We started early the next morning, but we were hindered much by the shallows. We pushed for an hour or so in one place. Katherine gave us some cold chicken and coffee which gave us the extra strength we needed, so we managed to push free and continued down stream arriving at the oil company port in the afternoon. We found our belongings on the bank covered with our tarp. From here we walked to the pista which is about an hour walk from the river and returned. Parker Company workers had moved in there since Bro. Marvin, Mario, and I had flown over checking the pista. I obtained permission for Bro. Marvin to land here and we returned to the boat on the river.

The next day, Sunday, we had our services on the bank of the river. I felt the Lord's nearness in this service which gave me the reassurance He is ever with us.

Monday is the day Bro. Marvin is to come for the first landing at this strip. He does not know whether the landing strip can be used or not. We had made our plans in Santa Cruz before I left we would clean off the strip, and if it could be used, I would place a white sheet out on the end of the strip where he was to land. If things were not favorable for a landing by this Monday, then he would return in two days (Wednesday). We walked to the strip, cleaned it off a bit, and I stood by until about 1:00 p.m. when I heard the sound of a motor in the distance. Marvin saw the sheet and put down. After greetings and mail call we saw Rolando coming from the woods with a large fish, probably 25 or 30 pounds. We all walked back to the river for refreshments and a snack and as time was getting by pretty fast, Marvin, Katherine, Mary Jane, and I walked back to the pista. Mary Jane had come with us this far because she had Easter week off from school and wanted to be with us. Now she would be leaving us to return to Santa Cruz. I suppose this was the first time in her life we would be separated as a family. As they took off from the airstrip, we waved goodbye as they disappeared into the distant sky. What a marvelous day that will be when we are all caught up together—*"And so shall we ever be with the Lord."*

Katherine and I now began our walk back to the boat on the river. The insects seem to be a constant menace to Katherine. She told me she thought she had been bitten more in one week than in all her life. There are ways, however, one learns to combat these insects. It is important to keep the body covered as much as possible, begin the day early, and go to bed at dusk when the mosquitoes are worse, always sleeping under a net. Then, too, one develops a reflex that helps combat them. Mario made a horse's tail out of motacu (type of palm) to fan away the mosquitoes. We use an old rag, towel, or whatever might be handy.

Camping on sand bar. Meat hanging up to dry.

A group came by boat for church service.

Chapter 2
A Battle with Storms, Floods, and Cold Winds

The missionary party camped on the Yapacani River at the last point where they could still have contact with Bro. Marvin by plane without a two or three day trip back up the river to meet him. The plane had already been a great blessing. They daily thanked God for the plane and for the people who made it possible. They looked forward to having radios later for closer daily contact with Bro. Marvin.

Katherine cooked on the boat, and they used it for temporary sleeping quarters. She had a kerosene stove which required repair from time to time. They put some of their equipment on the bank and covered it with a tarpaulin.

The next few days were spent in planning, trying to get as much information as they could about the area, probable location of the savages they hoped to reach, and doing some maintenance work on the boat. They were learning much about life in the jungle and travel on the river.

Bro. M. S. relates this event:

One Saturday afternoon we had gone up the trail and on returning about 5:00 in the afternoon I thought I saw water down the trail as far as I could see, coming toward us. At first I thought this must be a mirage—this just couldn't be—but then I thought of the turbions (flash floods) that are so common to these rivers in the orient and which are one of the unpredictable happenings of this country. It had rained toward the mountains the night before, and while we were only gone two hours, the river had risen almost four feet. We didn't know if we would find the boat and our belongings or not, so we rushed on, wading through the water coming down the trail to see if our boat was still holding. On arriving we found the boat swaying but still secure. However, the water was threatening our belongings under the tarp on the bank, being only a few steps away, and when I saw the situation, I fired three shots into the air to signal Mario and Rolando for help. They were still up the trail and unaware of the situation. Katherine and I started pulling down the tarp and moving some small chickens which were in danger to higher ground. Four chickens were drowned, but we were thankful to the Lord He spared our boat and equipment. By the time Mario and Rolando reached camp, the water had reached its peak, but we stood by for several hours to make sure.

Another storm hit the camp as Bro. M. S. relates:

One day we had a tropical storm. The storm winds blew everything off the boat that wasn't tied down. Katherine lost some clothes in the water. Later I found her big wash pan under the boat., and we found other things that had blown on the ground. The strong wind blew rain in under our tarp on the bank. We held on for an hour or so during the onslaught. Our boat, War Ark, was fast against the bank, so she stood well. The water began to rise again the following day and since the rains had stopped, Katherine and I condensed our cargo under the tarp and threw away wet boxes, etc.

On Sunday we had our regular services and in the late evening Carmelo came from down river with another man (this is the man who had helped us load our equipment on the boat one day) and stopped near our camp. He related to us a week ago, during the tropical storm we had, one of the three men in their party had gone to the edge of the river chasing a jochi (river rat,) and the bank caved in due to the rapidly rising and swift waters, and the man was swept away. What a pity! He had a family, but what is worse most of these people have no personal or saving knowledge of the Lord. We have not seen mass conversions here, but as we continue to preach the truth it gives us great joy every time we witness the repentance and conversion of a sinner. Carmelo and the man with him looked for the body for two days and finally gave up and started back upstream because their gasoline was running low.

Mario and Bro. Arrington went down river looking for a site for base camp—high, level, etc., which would be safer in a turbion (flash flood) or storm. They passed a camp (home) of a friendly Yuras Indian, his wife, and baby. They lived on the ground with nothing but a roof of "chuchio," which is the branch of reeds or cane that grows along the river. The little baby was swinging in a homemade cradle which almost touched the ground. The cradle was tied from one post of the little roof to the other, and the Indian mother would give it a swing occasionally. The baby, though the weather was warm, was covered from head to foot. That was the custom they observed.

The Indians had some meat, hides of wild pig and cats, drying in the sun on the far side of the river. They agreed to go down river with the missionary party about an hour and a half to investigate a high place they knew. It took about three hours to return to the camp upstream in the small boat. The friendly Yuras gave Bro. Arrington some dried chancho (wild pig), and the missionary party continued up river to their temporary camp.

Bro. Arrington tells of another change in the weather:

It rained again before day and about daybreak a "surrazo" blew in cold and strong. We live in a generally hot climate, but one of the strange phenomena of Bolivia is a surrazo. The wind blows most of the time from the north or northwest, but when the wind changes and blows from the south usually it brings a cold wind, with or without rain, and can be quite cold for a few days, and then it turns hot again. I took advantage to replenish our dwindling food supply. The Lord blessed us "filling our barns with plenty." I was able to get three ducks, a good sized fish, and later I went after a wild pig. I could hear the clatter of the pig's teeth as the dogs held it at bay. When cornered these wild pigs can be very dangerous to both man and beast and can kill a dog quickly. It is cold tonight for Bolivia. We are hovering around the fire.

Chapter 3
A Move to a Higher Place

The rainy season would bring more water and danger from flooding. They needed to find a more comfortable and safer place to camp. The following is the account of moving day as told by Bro. Arrington:

We left this morning, Monday, May 5 for "La Alta" (the high place Mario and I found previously). We are pressing closer and closer to the area where we will leave the river and enter the jungle by trail we will cut. The sun is shining bright this morning after the bad weather. Mario is up front on the big boat helping to look for obstacles, and I am at the motor which we have on the small boat, tied along side and pushing the large boat. One can see better this way at least on one side. The big boat was so crowded we couldn't see through it, and we were almost going in the blind so we changed our rigging. Rolando is on the opposite side on the big boat to warn me of any obstacle on the left, my blind side. Katherine is inside with her life jacket on. I think everyone was dreading this trip because Mario and I had told of our encounter the other day with obstacles. But the river was up some from the last surrazo, and we made it alright. One feels funny though going downstream pushing a large boat with a smaller one and not being able to see to the left—taking signals and having to do some fast maneuvering at times.

I think we were all glad and relieved to arrive at our new location. We put in at a curve in the river at the "high place." The water was deep right up to the clay bank that went straight down. I jumped out to help secure the stern and almost had to swim out, but managed to plant my hands firmly enough in the clay to finally drag myself out. Katherine and I put up a tarp shelter to sleep under on the bank. We have slept on the boat now for over a month, and it feels good to stretch out again. This was like a new house for us. Now we could keep some things dry since this tarp was five by eight yards. The other we had been using was only three by four yards. Katherine began sweeping the floors just as if they were hardwood. Actually, after use the floors become hard and can be swept as clean as a stone floor. I turned on my battery radio and picked up the contact of some New Tribes missionaries. It sure seemed good to hear the voice of the missionary of the New Tribes in Santa Cruz, with whom I am acquainted, speaking to others in the field although he had no idea, I am sure, we were picking him up.

We are now set in a temporary camp at the high place from which we hope to hold an every two-week contact with Bro. Marvin at the oil company pista (airstrip). The airstrip is about a day and a half to two days up river. The travel time depends upon the stage of the river. We plan to stay here until we can build our own airstrip. This is the farthest point so far, and almost nobody ever ventures this far into the jungle other than occasional hunters. We feel it is best not to move further down river until we have a landing strip nearer to maintain contact.

Any further distance from down river to the oil company airstrip would require too much time.

After arriving at the "high place" on the river we experienced the worst weather yet with surrazos, driving rain, and flooding of the river. We were busy trying to keep the boats, motor, and belongings safe. The river had risen about eight or ten feet and was steadily rising toward our camp. If the water had risen one more foot, we had made plans for all to go aboard War Ark and take on all the belongings we could and wait out the flood. Everything was wet, and it was hard to start our fires. I found an old oil can and put some small sticks and paper in it and poured gasoline over them. Then I covered the oil can with a larger can to keep out the rain. In this manner I was able to keep fires going through our worst weather.

First church built on the Chapare River. In background Bro. Jerry Kidd with son, Jason, Katherine, and Mary Jane.

Chapter 4
An Important Appointment

Bro. Arrington and the others were dependent upon the contact with the plane for mail, supplies, and emergency transportation back to Santa Cruz. Since they have moved to a higher and safer camp, they must spend several days going to and from the contact times with Bro. Loyd. Bro. Arrington tells of a typical trip:

Mario, Katherine, and I left on Saturday for a regular two-week contact with Bro. Marvin to receive our supplies. On our overnight stay on the river we put up on a bar for the night, but the insects were so bad Katherine went to her net after the supper was prepared preferring to do without her food than to fight the swarms of mosquitoes and other insects. (I took some food to her net). We had our devotions on the sandbar the next day, but we are going to talk to Bro. Loyd about changing our contact day that we might all be together in our camp on Sunday for our service.

We arrived at the landing near the pista about 3:30 in the afternoon and set up camp for the night on the bank. The following morning we walked down the trail to the airstrip to await Bro.

51

Marvin. Around noon we heard the plane approaching. One can just about set his watch by Bro. Marvin's schedule. Except for something unusual he is always on time. We all lugged supplies back to the landing on the river. The sun was bearing down. After a brief visit and planning Bro. Marvin headed back for Santa Cruz and our party of three got underway by river for an hour or so before dark and again set up our overnight camp. We could see lightning after dark in the distance and about ten o'clock it began to rain. Mario had not put up his shelter, so he had to join us. An anta (South American elephant) came crashing through the jungle near our beds during the night. The visitor, along with the rain and wind that often tumbles trees down, afforded us little sleep for the night.

The next day after we arrived back in our camp we began a search of the immediate area for an airstrip. There is a place across the river that looks good. Before we start work on a pista here, we are going to try to get to the campo that Bro. Marvin and I saw when flying over the jungle. A campo is a clearing in the jungle with short growth and often holds water. If we can cut through the jungle and reach the campo soon and can find a place dry enough, we might be able to clear a landing strip there. This would put us nearer to the Chori River and, we believe, to the savages.

Bro. Marvin and I have flown over this area several times trying to get a good aerial view. From the Yapacani River the campo is probably 15 or 20 kilometers toward the Chori River.

Rolando is having trouble with toothache and plans to go in. He has been having a great deal of pain lately. After seeing him off the three of us remaining in camp left on the 21st for about an hour's distance down river to investigate another high place on the river. Mario feels it would be better to cut through the jungle from that point to the campo and on toward the Chori River. On the way we gathered three dozen gaviota eggs the birds had laid on a sandbar. Mario says they are good to eat. We shall see.

Soon we arrived at the high bank we were looking for and began to check the area. We decided it was favorable, and we would try cutting from here in a few days. It was by now getting late and clouds were gathering, so we started back to our camp. Because of shearing pins we were delayed, and the mosquitoes were coming. We usually try to get supper and the chores done before dark because at dusk the mosquitoes begin coming. We could see lightning in the south which was our warning of an approaching surrazo. When the wind came, it brought heavy rain which blew under our tarp at our camp. One of our needs at present is to get better established in a base camp and build shelters.

Jungle Missions in Bolivia.

Next day on sand bar after Deek's hemorrhage.
He had a bleeding ulcer, but he refused to turn back.
He continued to run the motor.

Anaconda snake killed in front of our house.

Part V
Seeking the Savages

The longing of the heart of Missionary
Arrington was to reach the unreached, preach to
those who had not heard, win those who had not
been won, baptize those who would follow Him,
and organize a New Testament church. He tried
to contact a tribe of savages sometimes called
"Barbaros" by cutting into the jungle where they
were sighted, leaving gifts, and praying for an
opportunity to meet and minister to them. He
was warned by friends and strangers alike the
work was very dangerous. However, he trusted
the Lord to care for him and did not fear what man
could do to him.

Bolivia—Bro. Arrington's jungle mission on the Chapare River.

Chapter 1
A Search for the Barbaros

The story of the search for Barbaros can be best told by Bro. Arrington. The following is his account of the work:

Mario and I put up our shelter and nets and decided to cut in allowing ourselves time enough to walk back to our shelter before dark. One can walk back on a trail in a matter of minutes which has taken hours to cut. We had a "walkie talkie" radio with which we tried to hold contact with Katherine back at our camp, but evidently the tall trees of the jungle were too much of a barrier for our contact. We could not receive her signal, nor could she receive ours. The next morning Mario and I began where we had left off and we cut most all day. We were hot and tired and a long way from the river, but we drank water from bejucu. These are large vines that hold water. We also came across an old fallen tree that had rain water in a hollow. Although we kept on our compass reading, we were not able to reach the camp. We decided to turn back for now since we had no contact with Katherine back in camp. On our way out Mario got a monkey to take back with us. We traveled after dark and in the rain in order to return sooner back up river to our camp.

The next day in camp we celebrated our return from our first "cut-in" into the jungle. We had fish and a turtle cooked in its own shell over an open fire. At this particular time of year we are having bad weather. The river is rising and muddy. We are using lake water. As the river continues to rise, large trees are coming down the river. We pulled the boat back into a cove away from the logs and trees that were coming down and tied it good from bow to stern. The surrazo is still with us, but we plan to go back down river to continue our trail into the jungle.

On the following day Rolando and I went down river to start our walk to the end of the trail. When we reached the first little arroyo, we caught some little bony fish that were about three or four inches long. We would keep them to cook whole for our supper. We continued to the farthest point we had previously cut and made our camp for the night. Since we were low on water, we walked back to the hollow tree we had found before and filled our canteen. We began cutting again the next day and continued until it was practically impenetrable. In this encounter we reached a place that was so thick we were hardly making any progress. We had reached an area that convinced us the Lord would have us build a temporary airstrip near our present camp until we could get through this thick growth and investigate the campo as a possible site for an airstrip. We abandoned the effort temporarily and returned to our camp again.

On a trip up river for a contact with Bro. Marvin, we stopped on a sandbar about 4:30 to allow time to pitch camp before dark and before the mosquitoes would be so bad. Nearby behind a log we discovered three large fish apparently just killed and a bow and three arrows. We did not know what to make of it. Here we were in wild uninhabited jungle country. We reasoned this had to be Indians because of the barefoot tracks and the bow and arrows. Hunters that would come this far would wear shoes and use guns. We began to think it might be the barbaros who heard us coming and left hurriedly. We saw no one, only barefoot tracks leading to the river.

Here we were with this confrontation and I think of only yesterday when we were returning from down river where we had cut dense jungle growth trying to get closer to an area where we felt the barbaros might be. Yes, here we are on this bar tonight. The three fish, bow, and three arrows are still just a few steps away from us. Could this be it? Could this be the time we have waited, worked, and prayed? Would they be friendly? Is it a trap? We lay there on the sand bar under our nets and discussed the matter from every angle after making the discovery. We were thinking of what our move would be in the morning, and if this developed into a friendly contact, we must, for the sake of the mission, keep this secret at least until we could establish a more permanent contact. As we pondered these things, we heard someone approaching in a canoe. It turned out to be the friendly Yuras Indian. This answered our questions concerning our discovery, and the next morning with mixed emotions we continued up river for our contact arriving after dark, wet, tired, and disappointed, yet thankful to the Lord for His promise found in Romans 8:28. We set up our camp and it rained during the night.

Chapter 2
A Signal from the Jungle

The work of cutting into the jungles was carried on at every opportunity. Certain days were set aside to make contact with the outside world through the meetings with Bro. Marvin. They looked forward to those days as they would receive mail and supplies to enable them to continue their work.

Due to the falling water in the river the contact was taking more and more time and becoming almost impossible. There was great difficulty in getting the supplies back down the river. The greatest need was to cut out a new "pista" (airstrip) near their home. Bro. Arrington tells of the plan:

Marvin and I made our plans. He would fly back to Santa Cruz and try to hire three workers and bring them back to help me. They would walk back to the boat with me and then on to our camp and help me with the pista. I would spend the night in the Parker Oil Company Camp and wait for Bro. Marvin to return tomorrow.

Bro. Marvin came with three converted Guarani Indians who had agreed to work for one month.

What a blessing! I found out later Marvin had quite a time rounding up workers. No one seemed very anxious to come to work. We feel the Lord moved upon the hearts of these three men to help us. Marvin and I laid some fast plans for the next few weeks. We would break off our regular contact for one month while we tried to complete the airstrip near our camp. Marvin would fly over the site for our airstrip each Friday around noon for a visual contact. If every thing was all right, there would be no signal. If there were an emergency, I would have two white sheets folded in the form of a cross placed on the cleared end of our strip. When the strip was ready for Marvin to land, I would place a full sheet, unfolded, on the end of the strip where he was to land. On some of his trips flying over Marvin would drop our mail to us and he would try some drop outs of food to keep us going. After bidding one another farewell, Bro. Marvin was soon airborne again for Santa Cruz.

We began listening for the plane the day Bro. Marvin would be flying to check on us. About 11:30 we heard the plane motor. Bro. Marvin circled over us a time or two where we were working on the strip and seeing no emergency signal, he dropped the following note which was fluttering toward the river when Jeronimo retrieved it: "Brethren: All is well; church is doing good; Emeterio shows spirit of real Christian. Not much mail; will drop next time if no need for contact." Marvin.

By "no need for contact" he meant if there were no emergency that would require us to try to get out of here and meet him at the Parker airstrip. We were all a little disappointed at not receiving any mail but looked forward to the next Friday when we hoped to have some.

Another contact day came, and a surrazo with rain had blown in, but it cleared in time and Bro. Marvin came about 11:30. He flew over and circled us for a visual contact. Seeing no emergency signal out, he dropped the following note:

IS NOT POSSIBLE TO USE THE LANDING STRIP OF COMISION MIXTA (railroad workers up river). MUST RETURN TO PUERTO PALO. IF YOU NEED THE USE OF THE PLANE, PUT UP BOTH HANDS IF YOU RECEIVE THIS MESSAGE. DROP MAIL NEXT. MARVIN.

The railroad workers were building an airstrip about a day's distance down river from us. It would have been easier for us to make contact there because there was more water in the river, and the going would be easier downstream. However, Bro. Marvin was telling us we could not use this strip as we had previously planned. We all lifted our hands into the air to let him know we got his note. On his next circle over us, the mail was dropped. How welcome! We had wondered about the possibility of the mail falling in the river because it is so close to the airstrip, but whoever threw it out made a good shot because it fell right in the middle of our airstrip clearing.

We had previously prepared a sign made of charred poles we had cut and burned when clearing the airstrip. We arranged the charred poles to form a sign which read: FOOD - MEAT. Bro. Marvin saw the sign and made a large circle around our camp and airstrip clearing and was probably writing the following note which was dropped.

IF YOU NEED MEAT TODAY, STAND WITH HANDS DOWN; IF NEXT WEEK, WITH HANDS UP.

When I translated this note, it seemed the Indians understood my Spanish better than ever before because immediately all hands went down. I was almost persuaded they might have read the note in English, but I suppose it was because of their jubilance at the prospect of getting some rations and fresh meat.

The plane headed back toward Santa Cruz,

and we figured he would return in the afternoon with the rations. Bro. Marvin did return, and we could tell he had someone with him, and they began dropping out sacks of food. The sacks burst open due to the impact when they hit the ground, and we lost the rice, beans, cooking oil, and hamburger meat. The cans of salmon and milk were badly bent but were not broken open. A large piece of fresh meat and some charqui (dried meat) and oatmeal were alright, too. We were spared most of the drop-out and thanked the Lord for what He allowed us to receive. The impact broke open the hamburger meat, and it was stuck all over the bark of the stumps of several small trees that had not yet been cleared from the ground. Reina, our dog, did her part in cleaning up the mess. The beans were scattered over 15 or 20 yards, but we all got down on our hands and knees and picked up a mess or two.

On the following Wednesday, two days before the next visual contact, we prepared another sign made of charred poles in the clearing. The sign read: OIL - RICE - BEANS - BROKE. DROP ON BEACH.

At the end of this sign we placed an arrow, also made of the charred poles, pointing to the sand beach below our camp. We thought, perhaps, the soft sand on the beach would cushion the fall of the items dropped. On Friday, about the usual contact hour, our party of six, which consisted of the three Guarani Indians, Katherine, Mary Jane, and I, left our pista work to go down to the beach below us to await the plane. At the beach we put down the following sign which we made of green chuchio leaves: Pista Friday—meaning we hoped to complete the pista (airstrip) by the next Friday. Then we made the following sign which we made out of dark wet dirt and placed against the background of the white sand: SUGAR - OIL - FLOUR - MILK - RICE - BEANS - MEAT.

This was our needs for the coming week, and

if we could receive this by dropout, we felt we could make it until we could complete the airstrip. We also made a bulls eye of green chuchio leaves and placed it on a soft stretch of sand thinking this would be a better place for the dropouts to fall.

Bro. Marvin was always on time, usually coming about 11:30, but we waited until about 1:00 p.m. and returned to our camp. If things didn't go according to schedule, we never knew just what the situation might be. We finally decided Bro. Jurl Mitchell and family had arrived in Santa Cruz and Bro. Marvin might be waiting for Bro. Mitchell to get out of school to fly with him. We returned to the beach in the afternoon and before long we heard the plane. We couldn't tell very well but it appeared Bro. Marvin had two passengers with him They circled the airstrip clearing and evidently read our sign because they flew on over the beach. They circled over the jungle a time or two, dropped down, and came in low over the beach. It seemed someone was trying to drop a good sized bag out the door, but it jammed as the wind pressure forced the door back. Just before the plane cleared the sand bar and reached the river, someone managed to kick the bag free, and it fell a good way from us but short of the river. The bag had a large piece of fresh meat and some charqui and yuca in it. The bag broke, and the yuca broke in pieces, but we gathered up the fragments and used them. The meat was intact. Evidently they could read our sign on the beach because Bro. Marvin gave us the traditional salute as he dipped the wings and soared out again over the jungle and back toward Santa Cruz.

As the days passed our food supply dwindled, so I took to the jungle in search of meat. One day I wandered too far without cutting a trail and had to walk out by compass through thick growth. I was going in a general direction but missing our camp about two bends up river. When I reached the river, it was sundown and getting dark fast, so I decided to wade or swim, as the case could be, down the middle of the river back to our camp. When we were without meat I was nearly always able to get something. Once I killed a tejon (badger) and a melero. Now this melero, to me, looked and sounded like a panther, and I didn't think the Indians would want to eat it, but I thought I would ask them anyway and their reply was, "S-I-R-V-E"! Which means "YES! It's good to eat"! But frankly, these fellows eat just about anything that crawls. And what's more Katherine and I found ourselves being less particular all the time.

Carving an airstrip out of the jungle was hard work. After many weeks of back-breaking work, cutting, and clearing Bro. Arrington and his helpers were getting anxious. Only five days more to work and the last effort was to remove a large log that had washed up during a flooding of the river. They had to cut the log nine times in order to roll it away with poles, piece by piece.

The day they had been praying for finally came. He gave this account of that day:

We were all tense. This was a great burden on my heart because I felt the responsibility of having the airstrip in good shape and ready for a landing. For several nights I lay awake thinking about the pista. Is it long and wide enough? Is the surface smooth enough, and is the soil firm enough?

We had prayer and I put out the sheet on the south end of the strip which was the signal to land. Soon we heard the motor of the airplane, and Bro. Marvin, seeing the signal, circled and came in for a landing. He could not have made a prettier landing. The Lord had blessed our efforts, and we were now one step closer to the Indians. Due to the lay of the land our airstrip, of necessity, was a little short but by clearing a little more toward the river for a better take-off, Bro. Marvin was able to clear the trees on the north end by a safe margin.

The Guarani Indians were anxious to get out as they had been helping us now about five weeks. Mary Jane needed to get out, too, as her school in Santa Cruz had started a week ago.

Bro. Marvin relayed the Indians, and Mary Jane out to the Parker Oil Company airstrip. He would be able to fly two at a time to Santa Cruz.

Now that we had our airstrip, we would not have to make the trips back up river to the Parker airstrip for contact—we could now start checking on the steps necessary to buy and use short wave radios.

The end of a long day on the Chapare River, Bolivia, South America.

Chapter 3
A River was our Goal

On Monday, January 26 (1970), Jeronimo and I went back into the jungle. It rained hard during the night, and we got wet, blankets and all. We stayed wet for most of four days. By Wednesday we finally cut through the low, marshy swamp which had thick tangled growth, to higher ground. While in the swampy area I saw a large snake which scurried out of range, and Jeronimo killed a tarantula. While in a low marshy place we heard a loud hissing sound which may have been one of the large snakes we have heard about. We weren't hunting snakes, so we didn't look farther.

Having cut through the dense jungle growth to higher ground, we felt sure we could reach the Chori River before long now. We walked out again to our base camp for our Friday contact. Katherine and Genaro had been in prayer for us because they knew we were nearing the Chori River where the barbaros have been known to roam. Reina, our jungle dog, gave us the usual welcome by jumping all over us.

A few weeks later another attempt was made to cut into the jungle. This time Bro. Marvin and

two new workers, Daniel and Segundo, Guarani
Indians, went along:

We fixed our packs and early on the morning
of Thursday, February 12 we started out. After
reaching the swamp, we trudged for $3\frac{1}{2}$ hours in
water that covered the floor of the jungle. While
in this, we heard a sound that resembled the
sound of rushing, turbulent waters and feared
another avalanche of water was coming upon us
deep in the jungle, but later we decided it was
probably an Anta or Tapir (South American
Elephant) crashing through the thick growth.
After $7\frac{1}{2}$ hours of walking with full packs through
our previously cut trail, we reached higher ground
again. Here we put up our camp for the night.
Again, as usual, the Indians said, "No va a
llover" (it's not going to rain), and we had a
violent storm. The Indians were not accustomed
to put up a piece of plastic for a shelter, and they
got soaked. Lightning and thunder bolts were
crashing near us throughout the night and no
one slept much. I put my shelter too close to the
largest and tallest tree in the area for comfort,
and I suppose it was here I was best able to put
to use the predestination theological views, but
anyway, the Lord blessed us, and we were able
to set up a temporary camp the next day.

Daniel is the younger Guarani with us and is
rather quiet and does not have much to say.
Segundo is the older, being 42, and mumbles
quite a bit. I believe his speaking is about one-
half Spanish and one-half Guarani. It is difficult
to understand him. He was once uncivilized
and had long hair over his shoulders and a hole
in his lower lip with a bone or some sort of object
in the hole.

We cut in farther. I killed a snake in our path
with a machete. We encountered some more
water but not as much as we found in the swamp.
The next day, Sunday, we rested, had prayer,
and Bible study. There are many jungle sounds
when one is still and listens.

We moved our camp up on Monday. It rained hard again. The Indians are talking about turning back. Daniel says the mosquitoes are sapping his blood. Segundo had gone deeper into the jungle looking for game and came running back mumbling in his own dialect, "artos tigres" (a lot of tigers). We all had a big laugh out of this. It was serious yet comical. I told them it was dangerous to turn back now, and we had rations set up for our advance and for them to turn back alone would be an added danger.

On Tuesday, we penetrated the thick growth farther and crossed an arroyo which led us to believe we were nearing the Chori because we had noted it on our map. At the end of the day we returned to our camp for the night. It rained again during the day, but back in camp we were able to start fires and cook supper. Later Bro. Marvin and I took a bath in the swamp water and washed our clothes. We enjoyed this very much after a hot sweaty day in the jungle. In camp after dark one of the largest ants I have ever seen bit me and hurt worse than any other. It pained me for several hours and swelled. Insects, night birds, alligators, and tigers take turns, then in unison, offering us nightly choruses. The Indians were mumbling in Guarani again in their hammocks but were staying with us.

Wednesday, we moved our camp up to the farthest point. The mosquitoes were getting worse as the days passed it seemed. There was no water near, so Bro. Marvin and I dug down in the earth in what looked to be at one time a low place holding a little water. A little ways down, muddy water began to seep in, but it was water and with a few purifying tablets we had fair water for drinking and cooking.

Thursday was the day! About 11:00 a.m. we reached the Chori River. What a beautiful sight! We thanked the Lord. It had taken a long time through thick growths and swamps with water and tangled vines to reach this river. We had made many trips in, week after week, advancing slowly but steadily ahead. This last trip we reached the Chori in eight days. I was sorry Jeronimo was not able to go with us on this last leg of the trip. He had been with me on all of the others. We were now a long way from civilization but thankful for having arrived at this destination. We took a bath in the cool water, rinsed our sweaty clothes, filled our canteens, built a shelter for our kitchen where we would move up the next day, and left machetes hanging on the trees as gifts. We had prayer and returned to our camp of the night before.

In addition to the bees and mosquitoes which we left, we found a colony of ants taking over everything. The next day we moved our camp up to the Chori and on the morning of Saturday, February 21, we started across the Chori River. In the sand on the other side we found broken pottery fashioned by the Indians with designs around the top. We crossed to the far bank and found an old abandoned trail. We followed it for a while, up and down, but it grew dim. We then cut in for another hour at 300 degrees without success. We returned to the river, took our Saturday evening bath, and ate fruit from the overhanging trees. The following day, Sunday, was our day of rest and prayer.

On Monday we awoke to piercing sounds louder than any circus animal you have ever heard. We thought they were tigers but later learned they were Manechis, large monkeys with special voice boxes to make these sounds. We went up river about a mile and explored the old trails and finding nothing new, we returned. That night we heard sounds which we thought were people, but finally decided they must be from a night bird. They were identical to the sound of a human voice.

On Tuesday, our rations were down to dried beef and rice. Even though we did not encounter the Indians themselves, we gained valuable information which will enable us to continue our search on a long range basis from another direction where we hope to be working with a group of Yuras Indians. On the trail going back we came upon a tiger that was chasing some large birds ahead of us. We decided to push on across the swamp and get it behind us in the event of a rise in the water. Once on the other side we sent the Indian brethren back for swamp water. We bedded down for the night and read our Bibles.

Wednesday, we walked back to the base camp on the Yapacani River. Daniel seemed to be the most fatigued. He and Segundo will stay in camp a week and work on the pista with Genaro.

Roberto with his most faithful family in the church.

Chapter 4
A "Cut In" to the Jungle

Several years have passed since chapter 1. The Arringtons went to the states for a year's furlough. Upon their return they had a great deal of repair and rebuilding to bring the clinic and house back into shape. By this time they had short-wave radios, and Bro. Jerry Kidd and "Wings of the Wind" were helping with communication. They made many trips to cut in to the jungle. This one is typical of their encounters:

Two or three mornings we awoke to cloudy skies and lightning, but we continued upstream one time for two or three hours, tied up against the bank, awaiting the worst of the heavy rain and strong winds to pass.

Roberto and Bilma sleep on the ground on the high bank. The river is out of the banks in places. Katherine and I sleep on the boat. Every morning we put up the antenna and hold radio contact with Santa Cruz. Things are alright there.

We are heavily loaded and have supplies for a month . . . gasoline, oil, staple food, etc. It has rained a lot, but provisional shelters of bamboo or palm branches are erected to keep a fire going and to give the dogs some relief from the rain, mosquitoes, and other insects. Both Roberto and I have been stung by an ant, nearly an inch long, called "toucandero" whose sting lasts for hours. We are faring fine, however, with fish, deer, duck, and turkey to eat. We arrived at our first camp on the Ibabo River deep in the jungle. The next day we crossed the river to the old barbaro camp where we had cut a trail and left gifts before. The gifts were gone, and we saw where the barbaros had broken branches, which is their custom, as they passed through the jungle. This was encouraging.

The next day while studying maps, I noticed super market ads on the corner of a newspaper where the map was glued. I drew a mental picture of food displays, busy throngs shopping, etc. We had a birthday supper (mine, January 23) of deer meat and a chocolate cake made on an open wood fire.

On Sunday we had our services. In the evening Roberto was at the edge of the bluff overlooking the river. All of a sudden he seemed frightened and excited. I asked him what was the matter, and he pointed to a rainbow in the sky across the river. He said it was a sign the Barbaros would come out. Later, he told us before he became a Christian he was afraid and would not think of doing a work like this, but he was not afraid now and would go anywhere to serve the Lord. Hallelujah! He said when we were in the States on furlough he would look after trails for us. How we rejoiced at his spiritual growth! Before, such a commitment would have been unheard. To God be the glory! In the evening, under the net, we listened to tapes from Buddy, Terry, and Linda (our granddaughter).

On Monday, Roberto and I went 32 bends up the Ibabo in the canoe with the small motor to the mouth of the Chori River. Then we continued 12 bends up the Chori from where we cut trail into the jungle and left gifts. Katherine and Bilma stayed in camp with the little metal house boat (War Ark II) for added security. We arrived back at camp before dark.

We left camp No. 1 going upstream to the Chori River to establish camp No. 2 near the trail we had cut where we left gifts. We stopped in a bend of the river which flows on both sides of the camp. This gives us protection from three sides. We cleared ground and dropped trees for about 25 yards all around us for added protection. We saw signs where the Barbaros had broken branches that seemed of recent date. We were all excited!

We are a long way from civilization here on this little river, but this is where we must come . . . *"to the uttermost part"* in order to be obedient and to work toward a contact with the savages. Thatch roof shelters have been put up—one for a sleeping shelter and one over our fire. Trails have been cut for about five or six kilometers near both camps, and gifts have been left. We will be returning to the Chapare mission for contact with Bro. Jerry to receive supplies, receive and send mail, and visit with the members there before returning.

Another trip was made a little later.

We left the Chapare on February 22 (1976). It began raining that day and rained every day for eight days. Making camp at night was difficult because of the rain, high banks, mud, and mosquitoes. Roberto went with me to the first trail. We cleaned the trail and left new gifts. The old ones were gone. Due to the sickness of Roberto's little girl, he felt he needed to turn back so that meant Katherine and I would need to return for more workers. After securing the help of two Yuracare believers, we left again on March 21.

The first day and a half of travel was difficult because the little Ibabo River had fallen and was getting more narrow. We made it to the first camp on Saturday, March 25 . . . four days.

There were many insects, especially bees. They covered us. On Sunday we observed the Lord's Day with our Yuracare brethren.

Monday, March 27: One of the workers and I went across the river to cut trails and to leave more gifts. The next morning we all left going upstream to our second camp and trail on the little Chori River. The going was bad because the river had continued to fall, leaving many protruding logs. We arrived at our camp in the afternoon to find it covered with two year's jungle growth. The bank was steep, but we cut out steps to get up, hauled up water, gathered firewood to cook supper. Being hot and tired, we put up our shelters and nets and went to bed. The next day we began clearing off the jungle growth, dropping large trees near us. Plenty of staple food had been brought along and our meat from the jungle included wild pig, duck, and a variety of fish, including the piranha which, incidentally, is delicious! We built several shelters including a kitchen by using poles and palm branches. Katherine and I brought along a tent, but we were unable to sleep well because of the marihui, a small blood-sucking insect that came through the mesh.

Daily radio contact was held with Bro. Jerry in Santa Cruz, and we planned a drop-out. This meant flying over the jungle, finding our camp, and dropping items out of the plane to us. This is more difficult than it sounds. The drop-out was planned for Friday, March 31, but it was thundering and lightning all the night before and at dawn on Friday it was raining. We planned the drop-out for the next day. Our antenna was not working properly and contact had been bad. Bro. Jerry planned to drop out another antenna for us.

Saturday, April 1: Radio contact at 7:00 a.m. Bro. Jerry plans to fly today. In the early afternoon we heard the plane approaching us over the jungle. After several passes over us, the drop-out began. Everyone was stationed safely for the drop. Katherine was in the metal boat. The drop-out consisted of the radio antenna, mosquito netting to go over the mesh windows of the tent, rubber boots for one of the workers, mail which was most welcome, (even my income tax return), vegetables, a fresh chunk of meat, and a special treat from the Kidds (apples and candy). There were seven bundles in all, and the workers had a great time retrieving them from the jungle. We thank Bro. Kidd and his son, Jason, and a brother by the name of Dave Seaton who were up there doing the work. When we had all the bundles together and were opening them Katherine said, "This seems like Christmas."

Monday, April 3: We went up river a few bends away from our camp to the second trail where we plan to do most of the work toward the contact.

After cutting in and leaving gifts on the trail, we returned to the Chori Camp. Usually, we get enough meat for our needs while traveling between our camp and the trail. The wild pig is plentiful, and several ducks were taken. Katherine is making a pillow from the duck down.

While in camp we put up more shelters. One shelter was for our radios, batteries, and miscellaneous items. The workers built a shelter for themselves after my urging them to do so. Many times they wait until it begins to rain, and their beds and other things are drenched. Firewood was cut and carried to the kitchen. There are many chores to be done, and all hands are needed. Washing clothes is done by hand, and water must be hauled up the high bank.

Time was approaching for us to go back to the Chapare for a meeting with Bro. Jerry. The little river had fallen, and we had to cut some logs that had fallen and blocked our way. The chain saw has been a blessing.

One evening we came upon two or three trees that had fallen across the little river. It would take us a day or two to cut through the tangle. There were about three or four feet left for passing on the left side, but there was only an inch or two of water, so we were blocked. We caught fish for supper and roasted a wild duck we had killed. We prayed that night for help, and all got under mosquito nets and went to bed. The first thing I did in the morning was to look over at the shallow passage, and the river had risen during the night just enough for us to pass through. We praised the One who made it possible.

After taking care of correspondence and buying necessary supplies (in Santa Cruz), we left the Chapare going back to the Chori contact work. The brethren gathered at the river bank to see us off and promised to pray for us.

We made camp on a sandbar for the first night. The young Yuracare brother who, along with his wife, went along as a helper, heard a tiger back in the jungle and became excited. The tiger hide is valuable, and the Yuras kill them when they can.

Traveling was getting harder now. It was now five days since we left the Chapare mission. Dark was coming upon us, and we found no place to put up for the night. Just before dark we rounded a bend in the river and there was a small sandbar, but even so we were thankful. We have to put up nets, and it is really difficult to do so after dark with the mosquitoes.

We checked the trail at our first camp and saw bare footprints. That was the only encouraging sign we saw.

On the morning of June 7 the radio was neither transmitting nor receiving. We travelled on until about 10:30 that morning and arrived at our second camp which is on the Chori River. As soon as we could, we prepared a sign made of poles from the jungle, which read: R A D I O, indicating our radio was not working. We knew since Jerry had not heard from us for two days, he would be flying over before long.

It was Friday, June 9, about noon when we

heard the drone of the engine of "Wings of the Wind," coming over the jungle. Jerry saw our sign and gave acknowledgment by dipping the plane wings. They made several circles and were coming in low. We figured they would be making a drop-out. As they came over a small package with strings and a streamer attached was thrown out, but the string caught on the wing stout or wheel.

Another pass or two, and they were coming in low again. I signaled everyone to be on the alert. Another package tied to long strings and a streamer was released. It fell in the river. I sent the Yura brother on the run to see if he could find it. He couldn't. I hurried down the bank and down river and saw a small object bobbing in the water. We retrieved it and it read: "We have C. B., try Channel 1. If all is well have everyone stand by "RADIO" sign and wave your arms overhead. Prepare for two supply drops.

We could not make contact, but we signaled we were alright, and we prepared for the drop-outs. We were having a hard time getting down to the river and back up the muddy bank through the tall grass and tangled growth. By the time I got up the bank, the plane was making another pass for a drop-out. It fell across the river, and the brother wouldn't hit the water for fear of the piranhas, so it took us a while to get the boat untied and paddle across. Finally, the Yura brother found the package and tried to throw it to me from across the river, but it fell into the river. The wife of the Yura was on the boat, but couldn't paddle or handle the heavy aluminum boat, so the package was floating downstream. I was trying to get my heavy boots off to jump into the river while Katherine was shouting, "Don't."

While the package was floating downstream, it came near enough to the bank for the Yura's wife to retrieve it. It was a duplicate of the other notes, so now we figured the first package still swinging from the plane was a duplicate of the other two. The brethren were dropping three

78

notes with the same message hoping we would get one of them.

Then came the main drop-outs. Both of them landed in the thick brush near the river, but we were able to get them. The contents were cabbage (ready for slaw), spinach, carrots, radishes, apples, and a hunk of fresh meat. We all gathered near our clearing, so the brethren in the plane could see us and we were all okay. Katherine held one dropout bundle up, and I held the other, so they could see we received them. Jerry gave the signal he saw us. The brethren made one more circle over our camp and then headed southeast for Santa Cruz and we headed for the kitchen (a shelter made of palm branches). It was stew and spinach for supper.

On Saturday, June 10, we went in the jungle to cut a mara (mahogany) tree to make a gaveta (a hollowed-out log from the tree) which would serve as a bathtub for Katherine. The piranhas in the river discourage one as far as bathing there.

As usual we enjoyed our Sunday services. We studied our Sunday School lesson, sang hymns, enjoyed the Scripture reading, and prayed. On Monday we went again on the trail. Katherine and the Yura girl went along and stayed on the boat while my helper and I went deeper into the jungle leaving gifts.

When coming back out on the trail, we planted some bananas and Yuca near the river hoping to draw the barbaros nearer. We were late getting back to camp and had to clean the pig I had killed on the trail. We have kerosene pressure lanterns which give a good light, so many times we work into the night.

The insects were getting worse, and clouds were gathering. Since both indicated a weather change we went about cutting and gathering firewood before the jungle became wet. The smoke is a great help to drive away the insects.

The next day, June 14, Bro. Jerry flew over in the afternoon. After making several circles he

79

dropped out a bundle by parachute with a note. The parachute did not open. The note indicated he was dropping a tube for the radio, but the tube smashed into a thousand pieces. I took the tube out of the radio I had been using and placed it in the radio he dropped which was cushioned by a large innertube. By doing this I was able to talk with him briefly before the radio went out again. The trouble seemed to be the fuse now.

He made several circles and had probably used all the gas he could afford, so he headed southeast again for Santa Cruz. We appreciated his efforts very much, but there was nothing anyone could do, so we tried to get busy with other things rather than dwell on the disappointment.

Early Thursday we heard a plane to the southwest of our camp. It passed going northwest, and we figured it might be "Wings of the Wind." About 4:30 in the afternoon we heard the plane coming from the North. It was Bro. Jerry. He circled and was coming in lower now because we had cut down more trees to the south of our camp. One bundle was thrown out, but it fell in the river. We retrieved it and found it contained fresh meat. Another bundle, containing radio fuses and a letter was thrown out. The letter was from Buddy, our son, and brought bad news about my mother. We prayed. I put a fuse in CPM 518 (our radio) and it came on . . . a comforting sound.

By this time Bro. Jerry had headed for Santa Cruz. I called "Wings of the Wind," and Bro. Jerry answered. I asked him to call Buddy by ham radio to find out more about our mothers. Katherine's mother had been really sick also. I thanked him and signed off.

Friday, June 16: It was cloudy and a light rain fell most all day, but we continued dropping the tall trees around our camp. We had set up a 2:00 p.m. radio contact. Jerry told me he had talked with Buddy, and my mother was still in the hospital, but her condition was more stable. He told us Katherine's mother had improved.

On Saturday it was dreary and raining. We kept a fire going under our thatched roof kitchen to keep dry and warm. This was the most cheerful place in our camp. Even Senor, our parrot, who was perched near the fire, seemed to be understanding as he bowed his head to be scratched.

Due to the rain upstream the little river continued to rise. Monday night was bad with strong winds, driving rain and lightning. Before daylight on Wednesday we heard an unusual noise, and I got up to discover the river was still rising, and the boat had caught under a fallen tree and was slowly sinking. We cut the tree to free the boat. The river was out of its banks in places, but lacked about two feet entering our camp which is on the highest ground in the area.

We went upstream to go on the trail and pulled the boat right up to the top of the bank where the trail started. There was water on the jungle floor, but we cut around the deepest places. We continued to see occasional "breaks" (where the Indians break the small limbs or twigs to make their trail) which indicated the barbaros had been in the area. After leaving new gifts, we returned to our camp and built a good fire to dry out. Lobo, our dog, was tired and stayed close to the fire.

Friday, June 23, it was time to head back to the Chapare for contact with Bro. Jerry, so we left, taking advantage of the high water.

Deek and Katherine in doorway of our jungle house with thatched roof—not quite finished. I had already put out green plants out of the jungle.

Our house in jungle.

Part VI
A Mission to the Yuracare

The Arringtons moved down the river to begin a work with the Yuracare Indians near the mouth of the Chapare river. The nearest post office was a week round trip by boat. Bro. Arrington had encountered the Yuras on an earlier survey. He and Katherine hoped to establish a permanent work with these Indians and at the same time, as time permitted, go back up the Chori river by small boat to check the gifts left for the tribes they had been looking for. He was determined to continue to look for the savage tribe, but on a long range plan. He was confident the Lord would give them the victory.

The work with the Yuracare Indians would also give Katherine an opportunity to begin her medical ministry on a larger scale.

Jungle kitchen with all of
their handmade utensils and supplies.
(Yuracare Indians, Chapare River)

Yuracare hut on the Chapare River.
The little girl is swinging the hammock
where her baby sister is sleeping.

Chapter 1
A Great Opportunity

Moving day came on April 13, 1970. The War-Ark was loaded to the brim. The small boat was tied along side to push it with the motor. They hoped to reach their new home on the Chapare River, near the mouth where it enters the Ichilo, within a week. They soon found that would be impossible. They were loaded heavily, and the route they had to take, many times to avoid the treacherous water and tree tops, was the most shallow which presented many problems.

In order to make water safe for drinking, Katherine would boil river water for a full 20 minutes. When it was cool, she would drain off the sediment, and it could be used for drinking. One morning Katherine was boiling water to filter for drinking purposes when her foot tipped the small portable stove, water, and all over on her leg and foot. She was wearing long trousers, so the burns on her legs were only minor, but her foot was burned with second and third degree burns. She dragged her legs in the cool river water to help ease the pain, used cooking oil to lubricate the burns, forced fluids so she wouldn't dehydrate, took antibiotics to ward off infection, and prayed. She spent several days in bed nursing a sore and very painful foot, trusting the Lord to heal the wounds.

The day finally arrived when they moved into the midst of the Yuras Indians. Bro. Arrington cleared an area near the bank of the river which the Indians had given them.

Katherine realized what a great challenge they would have for a medical ministry as they found many sick among them, mostly children. There was a need for children's medicines to treat upper respiratory infections, coughs, infected insect bites, antibiotics, diarrhea, and fever. All kinds of vitamins for children and adults were needed as were dressings and bandages of all kinds. The news quickly spread that the missionaries had medicines and help for them. The people did not have money except the little they received when they could sell some fruits or things they had grown. They were very grateful for the help the missionaries brought to them. Katherine relates several times the children came bringing two eggs wrapped up or some fruit for them. The Yuras wanted to help build a house and a clinic, so the men began clearing a beautiful place on the river for the buildings.

Chapter 2
A Day of Rejoicing

The missionaries were confident God had led them to this place and had a great work for them among the Yuracare Indians who had heard little about the Savior. Services were begun in one of their houses and soon reached about forty in attendance. Bro. Arrington relates the following:

We had been having good attendance at our services but had no professions of faith. We kept preaching and praying. Then on the memorable day of Sunday, May 17 we had 20 people to come forward saying 'I want to trust Jesus as my Saviour.' What a day of rejoicing! Those saved were from eight to 55, half of them were children and half adults. A little child came forward first, then the others began to come forth one by one. I warned those saved they would face persecution and temptation now they were Christians. Just the next day one of the young men who had killed a tiger and sold the hide began to drink and celebrate. He invited the others to drink. He was not one of those who had made a profession of faith. As a whole I believe most of these people will respond to the teaching of God's Word. Most of them are friendly and alert.

One afternoon they were gathered around our tent where Katherine had been dispensing medicine. Suddenly they looked up, hearing a sound. They heard it before I did. They said this was a wind from the south. This meant there would be a cold wind and within 30 seconds it came. (These surrazos bring cold air with them in the months of May, June, and July, which is the Bolivian winter.) They all left, and soon I heard a chopping sound which meant they were chopping fire wood. Later that night we visited two fires. When talking among themselves the Indians speak in their own languages— Yuracare—but with us, in Spanish. As we huddled around one fire I realized there were four languages present: English, Spanish, Guarani, and Yuracare, and it warmed us inwardly to hear one of our Guarani Indian workers say, "Hermana" (sister) to a Yura Indian girl who had just been saved.

About a month later:

This past month has been one of many blessings although not without its trials. The Lord has saved 12 more souls since our last report. How we praise Him! Pray for us, brethren, that we may be able to teach them now. One of those saved was an old Indian woman, the oldest person in the village, who is the mother, grandmother, and great grandmother of the Yuracare Indians where we are. No one knows exactly how old she is. In fact, many of these Indians do not know how old they are. One day when we were visiting and witnessing we came to where she was. I got down on the dirt floor beside her and read Scripture. She said she wanted to be saved. She accepted the Lord. We prayed. What a blessing!

Another of those saved was the old woman's daughter. This daughter is the wife of one of the chief men of the village. I remembered her from my first visit here. We had been praying for her. Most of her family has been saved, but her husband is still unsaved. Some days earlier he had passed our place going down river with a sack of rice on his shoulder and didn't return. His wife and daughter went looking for him. They found him drunk, and late at night when they were bringing him home, he fell over the river's cliff and broke his collar bone. One of them went for help to get him up. I went to check on him and gave him medicine. He was in much pain, and his shoulder was swollen.

Satan has attacked in many ways, but we shall continue to resist him and contend for the faith until the end. One little girl who was saved attends a little school for children down river at the military post. They were having some sort of program in recognition of some fiesta and the teacher, who is from Trinidad, told the children to dance. When the little girl who had been saved refused, saying she was now a believer, the teacher struck her twice with a chuchio pole.

Satan has used alcohol to tempt the believers. Those drinking pass their bottles and offer drinks to the new Christians. One man, whose wife had just given birth to a baby boy, carried a bottle in a sack over his shoulder. He said it was to have on hand in case the baby died! The baby is still living, but I doubt the alcohol is still on hand. His wife has been saved, but he is still unsaved.

We love these Yuras here and sometimes they amuse us. One Sunday I was preaching and thought I was getting my point across when one fellow spoke up from the audience, "Pastor, you've a worm on your shirt!" I am sure some of them are amused at us also. One day Katherine was washing. They heard the generator and stopped by to watch the machine as it agitated the clothes. They commented on the contraption in their Yuracare language. They probably thought the whole thing was a failure when the pump started pumping out the water through the drain hose on the ground, so they left, still amused. Another fellow couldn't figure out what the clothespins were. These people have always beat their clothes with a paddle and put them on the ground to dry.

We are trying to teach these people to *"Remember the Sabbath day, to keep it holy."* They pass in the path in front of our tent with wild hogs on their backs which they kill on Sunday. But those who have been saved are receiving the admonition to come to the worship services on Sunday and hunt on another day.

These people are grateful for anything that is done for them. Katherine gave one Indian girl a dress. She was so proud of it and wore it to the next service. They all come barefoot, but we are proud to have them come anyway they wish, just so they come. Katherine gave a pair of shoes to another lady. She looked at the shoes and then at her husband with such delight. It may have been the first pair she ever had. We have been giving the old Indian woman, the great-grandmother mentioned earlier, some warm food to nourish her thin, frail body. We gave her a blanket because she had nothing but rags and, due to this surrazo, the weather has been quite cold both day and night. She doesn't talk very well, but we could tell she was grateful because of the tears that welled up in her eyes. She just sits around a little fire all day and makes her bed down for the night in the same place. We try to visit and comfort her regularly.

The Lord has blessed us here in so many ways. Down river at the military outpost there is a little sawmill, and we are in the process of buying lumber from them and hauling it up the river to our camp on the Chapare. We have already started to build the clinic. This is an urgent need. Katherine needs a shelter to work in, and a dry place is needed for the medicines. We also have plans to build a church building large enough for anticipated growth. We are greatly encouraged by these prospects and Katherine's and Mary Jane's enthusiasm are running high over the prospect of having a house with board floors. All of these shelters will be framed and walled with lumber, but due to the overall cost, we will have grass roofs which will last several years and can be replaced.

Our work on the clinic building is coming along well. Some had asked how we were going to get to the top of the tall poles to frame our roof. Well, I had wondered about this myself, but one of our Yuracare converts solved this problem. He made a belt of peeled bark into which he put both feet and scaled the pole to the top. The roof is of palm branches but is a haven for bats. These bats are a menace to us. They are a type of vampire and have attacked our little puppy. When we go out at night the bats swoop down at us. They have been known to attack people. I usually wave my flashlight over my head which pretty well keeps them at a distance. I don't fear their bite so much, but they are a known carrier of rabies. This is why we take precautions. Our clinic and house will have a ceiling under the roof which we hope will keep them out.

Chapter 3
A Permanent Home

Bro. Arrington wrote the following account in December 1970:

Things are going well here. Our services are fairly well attended, and the converts seem to be growing in grace. I hope it will not be long before I will finish the clinic and house. As soon as the floors and roof were completed, we moved. We even have a bathtub now. One of the men hewed it out of a log. Katherine has also made pillows for us by gathering lint, a wool-like substance from the pods that grow on balsa trees. The building has already been a blessing to us because the rains have started, and we are keeping dry, and what is more, the medicine is better protected. Many come for medical help.

In addition to help these people physically with medicines, we are trying to help them in other ways. Katherine has a nice garden and has given some of the Indians vegetables and seed to plant. Some of the vegetables and seed are unknown to them even though they are grown in other parts of Bolivia. We feel these vegetables will furnish a great deal of the vitamins missing in their simple diet.

The Yuras love to hunt and fish but in recent years have taken to raising crops, mostly maiz (corn), yuca (mandioca), and platinos, a large semi-sweet banana which they cook by boiling or roasting in the coals of their fires. Their meat consists mostly of fish, jochi, wild pig, and antas. Fruits can be grown such as oranges, lemons, mangos, papaya, guayavas, lima (a sweet non-acid lemon), grapefruit, and a variety of bananas. Bananas and papayas practically grow wild. The refreshments are called "refrescos." Some of the most unusual are made by mixing a little 'miel' with water. This miel is nothing more than syrup made from cane juice. Back in the States I would never have thought of making a drink from cane syrup, but when one develops a taste for this, it makes a good refreshment, especially when one is hot and thirsty. Then there is a combination of banana and papaya well blended with milk and sugar added. I think their favorite, however, is chicha. This is made from fine ground meal of corn and water. If cane juice or sugar is available, it may be added. This chicha has caused us some trouble though because those who are given to drink allow theirs to ferment. We are asking the Lord for patience, however, and are seeing some results as some are being saved.

Some of the customs, though, we do not wish to change, and we find it gratifying as we adapt them to our own ways that we may be identified and accepted as one of them. Many times when one may ask where something is or ask for a general direction, they will point with the lips. This we have about learned to do, but it will take much more practice before we can utilize our feet as they do. They can pick up objects with their toes faster than we can stoop over and pick them up with our hands. Anyway, we wear boots most of the time to protect our feet from the ever-present insects. Our skin just does not have the toughness to resist the insects as wells as theirs.

At the beginning of the rainy season a few weeks ago we witnessed some pretty high winds with thunder and lightning as the clouds from the north and south just seemed to collide overhead. The two remaining balsa trees near us swayed to and fro with such violence we feared they would fall on our roof. We stood by for nearly an hour until the worst was over. The next day or so we set about chopping them down, so now about all we have near is banana trees.

Our jungle house has been a rather difficult task, but I have it just about completed now. This is a great improvement for us after living on the ground, under a tent, for about a year and a half.

The work of the missionaries went on as usual in spite of circumstances, pests, and weather. Bro. Arrington relates more of their experiences:

The mosquitoes seemed to be getting worse by the day. We thanked the Lord for those who came to the service in spite of the mosquitoes. It is a custom for the people to bring a rag with which they do battle with the mosquitoes. Genaro got some posetacu, which are dried ant houses that the ants build in the trees and started them smoking. He then set them about our group to smoke away the insects. Katherine plays the accordion for us, but it was getting almost impossible for her to play because of the mosquitoes, so she came out with rubber gloves on and a mosquito head net, much to the amusement of the Indians, and played right on. The Lord blessed, and six were saved in the service.

Katherine had been treating one of the Yuras women. The woman was improving, but her husband took her up the Chapare, and she steadily grew worse. He took her to a "jungle doctor" but to no avail, so he brought her back in a state of semi-consciousness, a mere skeleton, and nearly dead. The Yuras man said she had been bewitched by a sorcerer, but Katherine immediately began a drip and injections.

I waited over at another hut where a Yuras man and woman were thrashing rice in a tacu by dim light. I could see Katherine in the distance under another roof working with the sick woman. Two of the Yuras women were helping her. Within a few days the sick woman began to improve and soon was taking nourishment by mouth. The Yura saw what a marvel the drip was and wanted to give her another not realizing she was given the drip because she was unable to swallow and take food by mouth. Anyway the patient is sitting up some now and talking. We praise the Lord, and we want all of them to be thankful unto the Lord and turn to Him.

Visiting with a church family.

Chapter 4
A Church Organization

The Primera Iglesia Bautista Misionera del Chapare (the First Missionary Baptist Church of the Chapare) was organized in May 1979. Those who assisted in the organization were Brethren Craig Branham, Ray Thornton, Jerry Kidd, and Manuel Torrico, pastor of the church in Santa Cruz. The church elected Rimberto Bruno to continue as their spiritual leader.

Bro. Branham wrote of his visit to Bolivia for the organization.

"Along with the Arringtons were Bro. Ray Thornton, pastor of the Parkview Baptist Church, Laurel, Mississippi, and one of his members, Bro. Montie Craft, as well as a number of the Indians and their leaders. A few yards away in a clearing in the jungle sat the Arrington home, clinic, and church building. By now the shadows were lengthening, and the people were anxious for the service to be completed, so some of them could begin their trek back upriver before dark since they had not brought their nets, a requirement for the jungle.

Through the years it has been my privilege to

96

sit in the organizational council of many churches, but this one was a little unique. A scant six years ago these people had been only semi-civilized and here in the deepening shadows of the jungle they were carrying on the Lord's business. Anyone who has attended the organization of a new church knows it is sometimes confusing for the new Christian to make the necessary motions at the right time in the right form, even if he has a Phd. The "motion maker" in this particular group felt it necessary for him to make everyone welcome and talk about the momentous occasion we were engaged upon at the particular time. My Spanish isn't too good, but I did see the humor of the occasion when near the close of the service Bro. Arrington left the pulpit, went down, and stood by the "motion maker" and said, "Now, repeat after me."

The First Missionary Baptist Church at the Boca de Chapare is our most primitive work, and one for which we can be extremely thankful. Perhaps, in no other country of the world and no other spot has the change from darkness to light been so pronounced as in the lives of these, our brethren and sisters in Christ

Some of those attending the organization of the
First Missionary Baptist Church of the Boca da Chapare.

Part VII
Hard Trials, Grace Sufficient

Illness, accidental injury, and sorrow come to all people at one time or another. The Arringtons were blessed with good health and safety most of the time, but there were several occasions when special grace was needed and received.

Chapter 1
An Illness in the Family

Mary Jane became ill with a high fever while the family was still living in Santa Cruz. Katherine took her to the doctor, and she stayed out of school for three days. She wanted to be with her classmates the few days before Christmas, so she returned to school on Thursday before the holidays but went home on Friday feeling worse. Katherine took her back to the doctor. On the following Monday, two days before Christmas, Mary Jane's skin and even her eyes began to turn yellow. Katherine suspected hepatitis, and they went to the doctor immediately, and his diagnosis was infectious hepatitis. She had to have complete bed rest for several weeks. She responded to treatment and was able to return to school after a few weeks.

After they moved to the jungle, Katherine became ill, but continued to minister to others who needed attention and neglected her own health. She finally went into Santa Cruz to see a doctor and was told she needed surgery. Bro. Arrington gave this account:

We went to see Doctor Bilbao in Santa Cruz.

100

He said he had a friend who was a specialist in the type of operation Katherine would need, so he called Cochabamba and arranged for the doctor to come to Santa Cruz where they would perform the operation. They scheduled Katherine to enter the clinic on Sunday, and her operation would be the next morning. I rented a house for three weeks, so it would be ready when Katherine was dismissed from the clinic. Also we were expecting our son, Buddy, from the states to visit with us during the holidays.

We bought up medicines for Katherine's operation. (That is the way they do it here. Each patient is given prescriptions and has to get them the best way he can and bring them to the hospital or clinic and keep them until they are called for). Dr. Bilbao and Dr. Tardia from Cochabamba came in about 11 o'clock, and Katherine talked with them. They took her to the operating room about 11:30 a.m. Waiting—waiting—waiting and praying. Marvin, Edwardo, and his brother are with me. During the operation Dr. Bilbao came out to give me a prescription and send me for catgut #1. I thought to myself, "What a time to be getting this!" I went to three stores and couldn't find it. I was, by this time, getting pretty desperate although I am sure I was the only one. They never get in any hurry about anything here. Finally I was told I could buy what I needed at a certain farmacia (drug store), but it was pretty far, and I figured by now they already needed it at the clinic. I rushed back to the clinic without it to get Edwardo to take me on his motorbike. We went for a wild and bumpy, ride to this store where I found the catgut. We made another fast ride back to the clinic to deliver it to the doctor. They finished the operation in about three hours and 20 minutes. Katherine came out about 2:40 p.m.

Thursday I brought Katherine home to our rented house. She is doing really well. We praise the Lord.

Katherine continued to recuperate at the

rented house. Buddy arrived so the whole family was reunited for a wonderful Christmas together. They followed up on Katherine's condition by sending her records to her doctor back in Jackson for his opinion.

Most of the time Bro. Arrington was well in spite of sunburn, insect bites, scrapes, and scratches from the jungle travel. He tells of an accident that resulted in a twisted ankle:

At the present time I am laid up with a severely twisted and aching ankle. Sometimes when the river is not too swollen or muddy, we leave a hook set out over night for fish to augment our meat supply and to divide with the Indians, who, at the time, may have no meat. Early Wednesday morning I had pulled a 50 pound fish out, and Genaro and I were bringing it up to be cleaned when I fell. The fish, almost dragging the ground, obstructed my view, and I slipped on the uneven ground. Katherine wanted to go down to the mouth of the Chapare and try to get a radio message to Santa Cruz in order to fly me out. I could wiggle my toes and felt that neither my leg nor my ankle was broken, so I didn't consent, however, I knew my ankle was badly twisted because of the pain.

It will probably be several days yet before I can walk. This is the first real injury I have suffered in the four years, and I thank the Lord for His watch and care over us. There is a purpose in this I am sure. Perhaps, I have been too concerned over trying to get things in readiness for our departure (for their first furlough). At any rate this has placed me in a position whereby I must trust everything in God's hands.

"I said, I will take heed to my ways, that I sin not with my tongue: I will keep my mouth with a bridle, while the wicked is before me. I was dumb with silence, I held my peace, even from good; and my sorrow was stirred. My heart was hot within me, while I was musing the fire burned:

then spake I with my tongue, LORD, make me to know mine end, and the measure of my days, what it is; that I may know how frail I am" (Psalm 39:1-4).

Also I have had time to muse and reflect upon the past four years and realize how wide the cultural gap is for a new missionary ,and how the Lord has blessed us to learn the language and see souls saved. Some things we thought to be so strange to us are now commonplace.

Indians on Chapare River in class with teacher.

Chapter 2
A Ministry, Treating Others

Katherine was "on call" at all hours, for one never knew when an accident or illness would occur. At times there were only routine medications to be given to the children for parasites, and at other times serious incidents required special courage. Katherine treated the ill without partiality. She gives a happy account of the delivery of a baby:

The month ended with a delivery. A man brought his wife by canoe. They had left their place about four in the afternoon and traveled all night coming down river. The weather was bad, and just as they arrived about 3:00 a.m., the rain began with a cold wind from the south. We prepared a bed in the clinic for her, and I delivered a baby girl at eight o'clock that morning. I was especially glad to have Mary Jane there to help me with the delivery. This was their first child, and both were very happy. This couple had lived here previously and had been saved in our services. The man was the one who had been accused of stealing before he was saved. I was thankful all went well because none of these people ever have any pre-natal care. Perhaps that accounts for the high mortality rate of new born babies here.

Bro. Arrington gives another account with a sad ending:

A Yura woman came down river by canoe and brought her husband and sick baby. The man had tuberculosis, and Katherine has begun treatment. These people wait, many times, until there is no hope before they bring their sick ones. They have their own remedies from herbs, animal oils, etc., and many still seek help from the "jungle doctor." The little baby died. One of the believers sent for nails to close the little box he had made from the wood of an old canoe. According to the woman this made the eighth child she had lost.

The little procession followed the trail that led into the jungle. A shallow grave was dug, and the little crude box was gently placed into the grave. This gave me an opportunity to comfort the woman and at the same time present Jesus to her in the few words I said there at the graveside. Many of our believers had gone up the river and into the jungle, but I noticed all present had made professions of faith except the mother of the child. We are praying and hoping she and her husband will be saved.

Chapter 3
A Political Crisis Causes Concern

Deep in the jungle the affairs of the government of the country were not of great importance. The missionaries days were filled with survival and ministry. However, one day Bro. Marvin brought news that would affect the Arringtons, and it came as quite a shock. Bro. Arrington wrote:

Bro. Loyd came in. We heard the plane and wondered why he was coming, since it was not a regular contact day. We headed down the trail for the pista. He told us the country situation was looking bad, and he thought the missionaries might have to leave on short notice. He also said he might not be able to fly back for us if things got worse, and they were ready to leave immediately. We had been listening to the news on our transistor radio, but had hoped things were about settled down. My burden was heavy. Quick decisions must be made. The thought of Katherine and I just walking out with nothing more than handbags and leaving everything else behind for outsiders to plunder wasn't the greatest burden. We had our mission, and it was young and growing, and I didn't want it to suffer loss or a setback. Then, there was Mary Jane in school in Tambo toward the mountains from Santa Cruz. I just didn't feel led to leave our work here with the Yuras Indians on such short notice. We had these new converts and building in progress. Many things raced through my mind. I told Katherine to go in and see about Mary Jane, and I would stay with the work and try to get it better established. I felt if we just walked out, or rather flew away, our work here would be lost completely or greatly set back.

We returned to our camp, and Katherine hurriedly packed two bags, and we returned to the pista. Our last words and agreement were that Katherine and Mary Jane would get on one of the planes the American Embassy had made available. I was told the Embassy had planes standing by in Panama to get American personnel out should it come to that. Katherine and Mary Jane would fly out to Miami. Marvin said he was going to try and fly the little plane out to save it and then go on to Belo Horizonte, Brazil. Of course, his family and the Jurl Mitchells would go out on the Embassy planes. Before leaving Santa Cruz, they would try to send me a message by radio to the military post. If all of this had happened, I had hoped to have our mission pretty well informed and bound together to carry on things there, then I would head down river to Trinidad and fly to Santa Cruz, check on things there, and see if any further word had been left for me. My next move would have been to try to fly out of the country by the quickest route. In tears we parted, and I watched the plane disappear into the blue. Some of the Yuras cried that evening in prayer service when I told them what had happened. They have learned to love Katherine.

Praise the Lord, none of the above mentioned plans had to be carried out. Things seem to have settled down rapidly, and Marvin and Katherine returned to camp the following Monday.

I told Marvin, it seemed our work was being shaken up pretty often, and I had decided if it happened again, if he could get Mary Jane out here to us, we were going to ride it out. We have too much at stake. These upheavals in the government of Bolivia are a continual thing and are recorded history. In the flare-ups sometimes there are from three to five men claiming the office of president within a 24 hour period. I do not want to leave unless we are actually forced to do so. Even then, I believe we will be given ample time to get out. Frankly, I have never taken these things quite so seriously here as some have.

The rains have started and this afternoon we had strong winds and rain, and the clouds are heavy. However, in whatever state we may find ourselves, we are happy in the service of our Lord and count it a privilege to serve the Lord Almighty and muse upon the words of Nahum, knowing all things are in God's power. "... *The Lord hath his way in the whirlwind and in the storm and the clouds are the dust of his feet*" (Nahum 1:3b)."

Chapter 4
A Separation Brings Sorrow

Katherine's arm became very swollen and inflamed, and she needed to see a doctor. Bro. Jerry was called, and he flew the Arringtons to Santa Cruz. Katherine was admitted to the hospital. The doctor applied cold packs on her arm and started antibiotics, but the swelling continued. A few days later a bone specialist was called in, and he advised surgery was necessary. Bro. Arrington rented a hotel room so they would be nearby after surgery for dressings and injections. The treatments continued for almost two weeks.

Katherine's sister in Mize, Mississippi called through a ham operator to say her mother had been hospitalized and was growing weaker. Katherine made plans to return to the States to be with her mother during her illness.

Bro. Arrington wrote:

"At 2:00 a.m. Saturday, January 3, the jet climbed out into the early morning darkness. It wasn't easy to see Katherine off, but we had prayed earnestly and felt, due to the critical condition of her 93-year-old mother, she should go. Of course, she wanted to be with her mother, but still she hated to leave. (We were elected as BMAA missionaries to Bolivia in April 1966, nearly 15 years ago, and this is the first time I have been separated from every member of my family. Our son, Buddy, was ready for college when we left the States; then about five years later, Mary Jane left going to the States to begin her college studies. Katherine and I have carried on the jungle work together since then until her departure for the States.) We have had several radio contacts by relay, and her mother remains in critical condition. Our family has always been a close-knit one, but God's grace has been sufficient..

After Katherine left I got about three hours sleep. Bro. Jerry flew me out to the Chapare about 9:00 o'clock. By radio contact I was told Katherine was admitted to the hospital in the States for further tests. I felt myself also to be in a difficult situation, but there was nothing to do but pray and I did that. By the next contact, Katherine had improved and was recovering nicely. It could go without saying this was a great relief to me.

I have continued with the work upriver, helping the "Yuracare" brethren erect the church building. By six o'clock every evening I try to be back at the radio just in case a message might have been received for me. Jungle growth between a laguna (lake) and the Chapare River has been cleared for the church site. The floor and most of the walls are completed. It is gratifying to see the dedication of some of the people. Oh, that they all were! Last Sunday as I sat in the middle of the group at the service (the women and children sat in a circle on the ground) I silently thanked God for what He had allowed and helped us to do as His servants. I remember a number of years ago when I left Santa Cruz striking out through the jungle by river, I earnestly prayed God would lead us to a group and give us a work for Him. It seemed so hopeless then in an unknown and wild jungle, but as I sat in that little group last Sunday I realized what God had done. He has been good to us.

Katherine's mother died February 16, 1981, in Mize.

M. S. and summer missionary with
Chapare Church after Sunday morning services.

Remberto Bruno, only pastor church has had; son-in-law
of Roberto. In photo he stands outside of church with
group waiting for others to come for services.

111

Summer Missionary Gary Ott 1974.

River trip.

*Maryjane Arrington Mathis
with Yuracare chief's wife,
Manra Elisa outside their home.*

Part VIII
Memories

The unseen hand of the Lord led the Arringtons to Bolivia and kept them safe from many dangers. The time came when it was His will to call Bro. Arrington home to end his labors. The following memories are given to summarize their work.

Chapter 1
The Arringtons Reminisce

Katherine muses:

Thinking back over our years spent there on the Chapare River, there have been many blessings as well as disappointments to remember. We have tried to use our medical ministry as a means to witness to those who would not think of attending a worship service. We cannot always know the results of a witness, but God's Word assures us of results according to His will.

A few days ago we had visitors who came from upriver. After talking with them, we learned the young man with them was the little boy who was bitten by a piranha about 11 years ago, and who came that I might sew his finger on again. He has grown up, is married, and he and his wife are both professed Christians. We had also witnessed to his two sisters and his father who said he trusted the Lord before he died. Thank the Lord for His saving grace.

Bro. Arrington remembers:

It was one of the most difficult times for me I can remember. Katherine had stayed in Santa Cruz while I had gone back for one last trip to the Chapare. At 4:07 p.m., October 8, (1982) I was flying out from the Chapare for the last time during the "phasing out" of the work there. Some impressions are lasting, and the memories will never leave. I remember looking out the plane window one last time and seeing Rimberto waving goodbye. The expressions on his face seemed to ask, "Is the pastor really leaving?"

During the two minutes in which I sat there in the plane while preparations were being made for the take off, my mind raced back over many years. I thought of the many times I made jaunts with Rimberto on the rivers, lakes, and into the jungle. Every day for them was a venture into the jungle as they searched for game for their families. Sometimes they would go to the lake for piranhas. Then in the evenings many times they would talk about the hunt. I remembered Rimberto telling how the wild pigs surrounded him, and how he barely escaped them by climbing a tree. Then my thoughts took me back to the little trail tunnelled through the jungle growth to our humble abode of many years. There in the early hours of the morning while waiting for the dawn, I would listen to the howler monkeys in the jungle and hear the heavy dew dropping from the chuchio and banana leaves. Waiting for the daybreak was always a time of meditation and prayer. I would think of the years the Lord had given us there, and I would ask His guidance for the future.

Then even little things, seemingly insignificant, rushed through my mind for which I was made to be grateful. How that I had been able to kill a large poisonous snake just off the path behind our house before it could strike, and how Lobo and I were able to kill a jochi (river rat) on the airstrip just when we were wanting meat.

After that came thoughts of the time Katherine and I were caught in the river. Sunday morning, September 13 during a surrazo. (A phenomenon peculiar to Bolivia.) Usually, it is hot and humid in the jungle, but due to a sudden weather change, the clouds from the south bring a cold rain which chills to the bone. The rain was so heavy I could not see ahead, so we tried to put in to the bank. It was so muddy we barely pulled ourselves up. We felt we would freeze before I could gather some firewood and find my waterproof matches. That was one of the best fires I ever remember huddling around. When the rain let up, we continued upriver to the church and were glad to be there for the service. We put up for the night on the bank of the river. I remember how warm and cheerful the fire was, and how thankful we were to get dried out and bedded down for the night under a shelter.

Then I thought of the sad times we experienced when some were taken from us, and how we would try to make a little box for the body and have a burial. I would plead with those still living who had made no profession of faith. Then I was made to rejoice when I thought of the many who had believed and were baptized. How I thanked the Lord when I heard Roberto say he didn't even like to smell alcohol on anyone anymore. How thankful I was when Rimberto said he would never turn back from serving the Lord and how grateful I was to see Honorato, who had been crippled, walking again and attending church services.

Then suddenly I felt the vibration of the motor as the airplane strained for the takeoff, and I found myself answering Rimberto, "Yes, the pastor is really going." While lifting out over the jungle and river and looking down on scenes so familiar, the rain began to fall and obscured our vision. But I could see the Lord knew best.

We arrived in the States October 29. It has been good to visit with relatives and friends again. We don't know what lies ahead, but the Lord does, and we are trusting Him.

Chapter 2
Mary Jane Looks Back

Mary Jane was gracious to provide a look at her experiences in Bolivia and to bring us up-to-date on her family and their activities.

As far back as I can remember my life always centered around church. Some of my first memories are of Sunbeams, singing choruses at the front of the church, and my Daddy polishing our shoes on Saturday afternoon in preparation for church the next day. On my fifth birthday I remember going to my Daddy's ordination, and from that point our lives really began to change. All of a sudden I was a preacher's kid and going to church every Sunday involved a long car ride to the church where my Daddy pastored.

When I was eight we moved from Mississippi to Jacksonville, Texas so Daddy could go to the Seminary there. While living in Jacksonville, Daddy pastored Ward Prairie Baptist Church in Fairfield, Texas, and once again we traveled about 75 miles on Sunday morning and then again back home on Sunday night. It was during this time my parents made known their call to missions. I loved living in Jacksonville, and too soon for me, our time there was up. Our lives became caught up with preparations for the mission field, I was soon to become a missionary's kid; I wasn't sure what that would mean to me but at the time, it entailed a lot of shots (immunizations) to protect us from tropical diseases, having a lot of dental work done, and a tonsillectomy. By August 1967 all preparations had been made, and we left for Bolivia. I had never been on an airplane, so that was an added adventure.

Upon arrival in La Paz and later in Santa Cruz, we were met with a whole new world. No one spoke English, and we spoke no Spanish. I felt like a baby. I knew what I wanted but didn't know how to let anyone else know! I decided then and there rather than make silly mistakes, I would keep my eyes open and learn as much Spanish as possible before I opened my mouth to try to speak it. When you are 12 years old you don't need to give people any extra reasons to laugh at you! Well, I spoke very little for a year. One of our first converts asked Daddy if I were mute! After a year I felt comfortable enough to give it a try, and I haven't stopped talking since! What a blessing to be bilingual!

We lived in Santa Cruz about 18 months, and then Bro. Loyd and his family came. Daddy had been building a boat in our back yard (now that's a whole story in itself!) so he and my mother could venture into our jungle work. The Loyds stayed in Santa Cruz and moved into our old house. I had been attending Santa Cruz Cooperative School for two years, and my parents and the Loyds arranged for me to live with them to finish my last year at that school (it went through ninth grade). This was the first time I had been away from my parents, and it was hard for me, but Daddy said sometimes there were sacrifices we would have to make for the Lord and His work, and this was my opportunity to show my love for the Lord. Of course, the Lord was with me and all in all, it was a good experience. The Loyds were very kind to me and made me feel a part of their family. The year flew by. There was a government upheaval during this time, and many of the Americans in Santa Cruz working for oil and government agencies had to leave. I had to say good-bye to many friends I had gone to school with for three years. Bro. Mitchell and family also had to leave because they were teaching in the school. We were very sad, but before we knew it, it was time for my ninth grade graduation.

I spent the summer in the jungle with my parents. I taught Sunday School classes and helped my mother in the clinic. In the evening since we had no TV (for that matter no electricity or running water) we would go up and down the trail visiting the Indians around their fires. Sometimes I would go with my parents and sometimes by myself. It was very interesting talking to the Indians about their culture and their life before we came to live among them. The women were the most thankful and would sometimes cry, saying what a difference the Lord made in their lives and in the lives of their families. It would make me ashamed because I took my Christian heritage so much for granted. I was so blessed to have been born to Christian parents, and I didn't always take advantage of the opportunities I had to serve the Lord! This was a wonderful time for me, although at the time I longed for friends with whom I had something more in common. The girls my age (15) were already married and had two or three children. I was thinking about boys and makeup, and they were worried about harvesting crops and keeping their fire going. Well, when it was time for school to start again, I found myself surrounded by people just like me! I attended a school called TAMBO that was between Santa Cruz and Cochabamba in the foothills of the mountains. The school was established by New Tribes Missions especially for missionaries' kids whose parents worked in the jungle. Spending the last four years almost like an only child, this was a very different life. I managed to adjust to living in a dorm and adhering to a very strict schedule. My life there was anything but boring, and soon after another summer in the jungle we were off to the States for furlough.

We arrived in Jackson, Mississippi after four years to a wonderful reception. Family and friends we had not seen for so many years were there to greet us. I felt like a stranger to everyone and everything. My life in Bolivia had been so different in almost every way, and it had changed me. The funniest thing to me, after we got back, was all of us would forget to turn the lights on at dusk. We would walk around in the near dark, and people would say "Why don't you turn on the lights?" Well, I guess we forgot we could! That year I enrolled in school for my junior year at Mize Attendance Center. I lived in Mize with my grandmother. Most of my Mother's family lived there and those in the small town who were not related to me had grown up with my Mother. It was a real treat being with so many relatives after not seeing our family for so long. The kids at school looked at me like I was an alien from outer space. Back then I thought I was just weird, and no one liked me. Now I realize these kids had no idea how to relate to someone who had grown up so differently from themselves.

I guess for me probably the hardest part of being a missionary's kid was not fitting in back in the States. I spent my year there doing my school work and spending time with my grandmother. I loved being with her and I have many fond memories now of that time. Because I had attended TAMBO which was a very accelerated school, I had all the credits I needed for graduation except two. I decided I would like to graduate a year early and go back to Bolivia with my parents so I would have one more year there before college. I would be able to spend time with my parents and friends rather than going back to TAMBO for another year. Graduating early meant taking two correspondence courses (English and

Government). I had plenty of time since I didn't have any activities outside of school and church. By May I had completed all of my studies, and I decided not to go through graduation ceremonies so I might be able to spend the last three months of our furlough with my parents visiting our churches. We went to California which was exciting for me. I had never been to many places in the United States.

In August after lots of packing and preparations, we were off to Bolivia again. I was so excited to go back to all my friends in Santa Cruz and to the jungle and the Indians. It didn't take long to get into the routine again, and soon I was teaching Sunday School classes, helping in the Clinic, and teaching in the school for the Yuracare kids. The school was located at the mouth of the Chapare River, and we hiked there and back (about a mile each way) every day except Saturday and Sunday for classes. This was very rewarding and a good experience for me. I also had an opportunity to spend some time in Santa Cruz. I lived there a few months before it was time to go back to the States for college. During that time I helped with the youth at our church in Santa Cruz and taught English as a second language at a school of linguistics.

My brother, Buddy, came down to visit in July, and he and I left together to go back to the States a couple of weeks later. He was getting married, and I was starting college. I remember being very sad in leaving Bolivia again after such a short time. The year had flown by. I had also never been separated by such distance from Mother and Daddy. I soon enrolled in Jacksonville College, and that became my home. During my time there I made many lasting friendships. I spent the summers in Bolivia helping with the work and visiting my family. Back in the States during school I would show slides and talk about the mission work from time to time. I was involved in the Mission Band, and we spend our weekends visiting churches and serving the Lord with them. It was at Jacksonville College I met my husband, A. Gene Mathis, and on December 17, 1976 we married. As the years have passed, I realize how God has a special purpose for our lives and each experience we have prepares us for the next. God gave me wonderful parents that showed me how important it is to serve the Lord at all costs and to seek His will for our lives. Even though my life growing up was so different than my present life, it prepared me for the ministry God has given us today.

My husband, Gene, was also reared in a Baptist Missionary Association church and was saved at a young age. When he was 16 years old he felt the call to the ministry and surrendered to preach. Gene was always very involved in Galileans and was the first Galilean ever to finish all the steps. God had been preparing us all of our lives to work together in His work. After we married I finished Nursing School, and Gene continued his studies and pastored his first church. We eventually felt God would have Gene study at the Seminary.

We moved to Jacksonville (again) and over the next three years Gene pastored another church (Damascus Missionary Baptist Church in Corrigan, Texas). Both of us always felt God would have us do mission work, and we both felt led to work with Spanish-speaking people. It seems every time we would consider a mission field, something would happen, and God would show us that was not the way He would have us go. Gene came from a large family, and we both enjoyed working with children. God led us to become foster parents during this time, and we adopted a baby boy. After seven years God showed us (or we started paying attention) our mission work was right at our feet. God called us into full time service with handicapped children. We now operate a habilitative group home for disabled children, the Mathis Rainbow Home for Children. In this ministry we are able to use our experience with children, our medical knowledge,

122

and our desire to work with Spanish-speaking people. We care for all races and ages and care for children who are ill or on life support systems. God has been very good to us and has given us the desires of our hearts.

Gene is also pastoring El Shaddai Church near our home in Alvin, Texas. In our home we care for 14 children. Our oldest son, Alton Slay, was born in 1977. We have three daughters: Shayna Beth, born in 1980; Sunnye Alyson, born in 1981; and Starla Catherine, born in 1987. Our other children range from 22 years to two years. Many we have cared for since birth. Over the years we have been granted custody of Mandye, T.C., Tye, Jordan, Jon, and Betsye. We are truly blessed.

M. S. Arrington, Jr. (Buddy) and his wife, Terry, live in Oxford, Mississippi. They both hold Ph. D. degrees in Spanish. Buddy teaches at the University of Mississippi (Old Miss), and Terry teaches at Milsap College. They have two daughters: Linda Diane, born in 1974, and Debra Ann, born in 1979.

Group on river bank waiting for baptismal service.

Chapter 3
Their Friends and Co-Workers Reflect

The following tributes were made by Bro. Craig Branham, Marvin Loyd, and Jerry Kidd, following Bro. Arrington's death. They are not given to praise the man but to call attention to the great God of that man.

My first recollection of Bro. Arrington goes back to Texarkana in 1966 when having been previously turned down by the Personnel Committee, he came back and earnestly stated, "God has called me to the Indians of Bolivia, and I simply must go."

My first visit with the Arringtons after they moved on the field came while they were still in language school, but after Bro. Arrington had made a river trip that had taken him deep into the jungle toward the Amazon. With maps spread out on his desk and excitement building in every sentence, he told me of his heart's desire for the work.

As a result of the deep burden Bro. Arrington had to get out into the jungle, the extreme difficulty in travel, the many dangers attendant to living that far in the jungle, the churches rallied, and the first airplane for the work in

Bolivia was bought as a piece of support equipment for the jungle work.

Through the years our ties grew stronger, however, one of the most enjoyable came in 1974. We were unable to get out to the camp where the Arringtons were living, so we spent several days in Santa Cruz in an old hotel the "Incas" had abandoned, at least it seemed that out-dated. It was during this time I learned of Bro. Arrington's depth of love for our work and his concern for his Indian brethren, his dedication to the cause of Christ, our association, and to missions, and some of his likes and dislikes of a personal nature.

Bro. Arrington loved our association and was proud to be one of our missionaries. He became angry when anyone tried to downgrade the work of our association. He felt no reason to bow before the gods of this world nor to take a back seat to anyone, for it was his conviction, and it is shared by this writer, with all of the shortcomings of our association, it is still the best in the world.

M. S. Arrington became known as "Deek" to me during this time, and our friendship grew to be very close. One can hardly think of M. S. Arrington without thinking of Katherine, who through the years, has been his constant companion. They came into Santa Cruz when it was a dusty one-horse town. They organized a church while they were still in language school, and, of course, eventually moved into the jungle. In the meantime the city had grown from the ox cart to the jet age in just a few years. The Arringtons always took things in stride wherever they were.

The longing of the heart of this man of God was to reach the unreached, to preach to those who had not heard, to win those who had not been won, to baptize those who would follow Him, and to organize a New Testament church. It was not the Lord's will, obviously, he should contact the tribe for which he had sought, but not being willing to sit idly by without witnessing, they lived for a year in a tent, finally built a house at the mouth of the Chapare River. Just about a year before returning to the States, one of the highlights of the Arrington's mission work in Bolivia occurred when the First Missionary Baptist Church of the mouth of the Chapare was organized. One of the great concerns even then was that the church would be Baptist...Associational Baptist.

Bro. Arrington is gone and along with many hundreds of friends and members of our association, I will miss him. However, scattered from here to Bolivia and back again are his footprints in the sands of time, and many of us will meet, no doubt, an Indian on the other side of glory, perhaps many of them, who will be there because of our ministry through M. S. Arrington.

Craig Branham,
Former Director of Missions

I met Bro. M. S. in February 1969. Bro. Gerald Price and I had just finished a ferry flight with the Cessna 182, and that afternoon we began a working relationship together in the Lord that was to last for many years. Bro. Arrington was one of those men in whom you could feel his missionary calling as you worked with him. For him being a missionary wasn't just adventure, or novelty, or a means to slip away to a foreign land for awhile. It was, as far as he was concerned, for as long as I knew him, the "rest of my time."

We walked many a trail, floated many a river, and slept wherever we were when the sun went down. We drank from whatever source was available and ate what we could carry or catch, and there wasn't a day he let someone else do his part.

Bro. Arrington had a calling to a type of mission work no one else in our ranks has had, including me, and he carried out his calling with real courage, faith, and a perseverance almost unreal.

I personally consider it an honor to have served with Bro. Arrington, and though my calling led to the Chiquitanos while his was for the Yuras and that unknown tribe, his spirit of missions has formed a part of my goal in missionary service. Thanks, Bro. Arrington and Katherine, for being a living part of our life.

Bro. Marvin Loyd,
Missionary to Bolivia

When the early morning call informed me Bro. M. S. Arrington had passed on to be with the Lord, I put the phone down and left the room. I had to be alone. No message I have received the last few years has had the impact of this message. I thought of David's words in 2 Samuel 3:38 *"...know ye not that there is a prince and a great man fallen this day in Israel?"* This statement is made, not to exalt the name or eulogize the man, for Bro. Arrington would not permit that, but rather it is to point out what God can do with one determined to surrender to His will. M. S. Arrington did exactly that, and it carried him to the middle of Bolivia's Green Hell. His going opened an era in BMA Missions that has not been duplicated exactly until this day. However, many new missionaries were challenged by his example, and work among the indigenous has flourished in BMA ranks since that time.

Our working relationship started in February 1974 when my family and I moved to Bolivia to work in the aviation ministry. For the next eight years we flew together for literally thousands of miles over the steamy thick jungle. We motored and paddled hundreds of miles in aluminum boats and dugout canoes. We cut and hiked through many yards of matted underbrush. Our beds were made on sand bars, on clay banks, and in the midst of the thick foliage.

M. S. Arrington was dedicated to his calling. I'll never forget one particular day on the river had been extremely difficult. The rains had fallen, and we were wet and cold. There was no sand bar to sleep on for the night, so we fought our way up a steep slippery bluff bank and cut a place out of the jungle. Finally, our individual shelters were erected, and I crawled under mine. Wet to the bone, cold, hungry, tired, disappointed, disgusted, and scared I began to think of my family in Santa Cruz and how in a week or so I'd be back with them. Then I looked across the campsite to see the silhouette of Bro. Arrington lying under his mosquito net. With conviction I thought, "I can leave this miserable work, but he can't. He must stay." And stay he did. That same night he called out across the camp fire, "Bro. Jerry, I'm going down to Baskin Robbins to get some ice cream. What kind would you like?" He had a tremendous sense of humor.

I learned he was determined to do his part. He was much a man and always took the lead. One day we saw smoke rising from the trees on the other side of the river. We thought it was the savages and decided to cross and try to contact them. I said, "I'll go first, then you can come." It was never to be that way. I'll never forget the picture of him wading the river, waving a white flag high above his head, and saying friendly words in the Indian dialect.

He believed Christianity would work among the tribes. He spent many hours in prayer for the souls and lives of the Yuras Indians at La Boca del Chapare. How discouraging it was to see them come to make a profession of faith and see some go back into the immoral world they lived. But he didn't give up. He preached the Word of God on Sunday and lived the Christian example before them during the week. The result was an organized church with a good number of baptized believers. One day I talked with Roberto, one of the first true converts, on the banks of the Chapare River. He told me how their life was before the pastor came ...drunkenness, untrue to their wives, not providing for their children. It was a miserable life. Then he turned toward me, and as tears ran down his hard, dark face he said, "But it's not that way anymore because 'El Pastor' has taught us how to live."

Jerry Kidd,
Former Missionary to Bolivia,
Assistant Director of Foreign Missions

Do the Yuras still worship in Bolivia's Green Hell?

Chapter 4
The Church Remains!

The greatest words that could be said of any man could not pay tribute to him like the work he has wrought through prayer, patience, obedience, and the grace of God. The church lives on! Praise the Lord!

The following article written by Bro. Jerry Kidd in the September 1987 issue of *The Gleaner* tells the story:

The twin engine Aztec circles slowly and carefully above the tops of the trees growing from the matted jungle floor beneath. Suddenly the semi-cleared airstrip came into view. It had once been the landing place that allowed access to the mission base of M. S. and Katherine Arrington at La Boca Del Chapare in Bolivia's Green Hell. The airstrip that cost Bro. Arrington and the Yuracare Indians nine months of hard labor to take away from the dense jungle, had not been used for six years. The powerful cocaine drug bosses had established their evil empire in this section of the Chapare and had ordered the servant class Indians not to clear the "pista" again. That closed the contact with the First Missionary Baptist Church of La Boca Del Chapare and their native pastor.

130

Subsequent flights above the area produced sights of the dark green wooden building with the tin roof being dismantled and relocated further up river as the nomadic Yura Indians changed locations. Now for quite some time no contact had been made and there had not been sightings of the Yuracare people. Words are inadequate to describe the feelings one has when he looks down on a scene such as this. The hundreds of man hours invested in the lives of the semi-civilized Indians are certainly the center of your thoughts.

What has happened to them? What are they doing? Have the teachings of the true God been mixed with the superstition of the jungle's mystic religions?

"Let's fly up-river." Hearing this request Missionary Pilot Larry Hendren turned to follow the winding course of the muddy river below. In a few minutes the fast moving aircraft had covered the distance that would have taken hours in the paddle driven dugout canoes or the low moving diesel powered river boats.

The river twisted and turned beneath us ,first to the left and then back to the right. Then all at once up ahead something began to take shape. There on the high-banked south side of the Chapare was a clearing with a number of grass roofed houses. There were the banana trees and the chacos (cleared areas) for planting rice, corn, and yuca. The river bank was lined with the handmade canoes and a large boat and barge was docked in front of the bamboo houses. Had the Yuras made a settlement? Was there any indication it was the same group that had migrated from "La Boca"? Then there it was, coming into view from behind the tall trees at the east end of the football field...a large dark green wooden building with a tin roof. The most predominant of all the construction on the river bank is the building of the First Missionary Baptist Church of La Boca del Chapare.

As the plane made circle after circle the people

gathered to wave. Once again the thoughts and questions came to mind. What is that building now? Is it a storage room for drug traffickers, a store, a school, a community house, or is it an indigenous New Testament church where God's Word is taught by a native pastor? I don't have the answers, but I prefer to believe the latter.

Bro. Larry Hendren answers the questions Bro. Kidd asked in his article in the March 1988 issue of *The Gleaner.*

I shared a little of my anxiety as I left Bro. David Flores and Bro. Freddy Mercado in Trinidad. They were boarding a riverboat to start the journey up the Mamore River to the Chapare.

The riverboat captain said, "Yes," he knew about the little village on the bank of the Chapare River. It was about an hour ride up river from the Boca (mouth) of the river where Bro. M. S. Arrington had cut an airstrip out of the dense jungle and established a church. The little village was now called "Puerto Ramanso."

When Bro. David and Bro. Freddy left Trinidad the second day of February for the Boca, the airstrip had not been used in over six years. We were not sure what was in store for them. They rode upriver from Tuesday evening until early Sunday morning. As the boat docked at "Puerto Ramanso," David stepped off. There was the little green building with the tin roof, and in the dim light of early dawn, a small group of people came to meet them.

Pastor Rimberto had aged somewhat, but David recognized him. "We had given up all hope of seeing you again," were some of his first words. Only the pastor's wife had kept up hope. (Rimberto's wife, Amanda, was one of the earliest converts in the Yuracare village. Rimberto was ordained to the ministry and taught sound doctrine by Pastor Arrington. He was conscientious in leading the church).

Pastor Rimberto shared this story a little later with Bro. Larry Hendren.

After Bro. Arrington left the Chapare back in 1981, the drug people began to use that area extensively for their cocaine production. Rimberto's life was threatened if they cleared the air strip off. Things gradually got worse until they virtually had to abandon everything they owned.

That went on for almost two years. They heard of Bro. Arrington's death in 1984 from a missionary with another group who was passing through. About three years ago they were able to move their homes the three miles to the new course the river had carved out of the jungle. Almost a year later the jungle dried up enough that they moved their church building too.

Pastor Rimberto had a tear in his eye as he said, "Even when we were living under the trees, we always had services on the Lord's day. And when our people pray, you still hear mentioned the names of Sister Arrington, Bro. Kidd, Bro. Loyd, and our other brothers and sisters. We have never forgotten to pray for you."

There are 20 adults and 23 children in Puerto Ramanso year around. They also have a school there now, and in the school year during the height of the dry season there are as many as 70 present for services.

Our visit was rather short. Pastor Rimberto had to leave on the riverboat before carnival, one of the most pagan festivals there is anywhere, caught him in Trinidad. We loaded up the Aztec absolutely elated. Jesus said a long time ago, *"Upon this rock I will build my church and the gates of hell shall not prevail against it!"* It hasn't, and won't.

Pastor Remberto Bruno; wife, Amanda; and children.